2943

An Immigrant Girl's Childhood in St. Louis

Millicent Petrov Shyne

Six Sisters Publishing

2943: An Immigrant Girl's Childhood in St. Louis

Published by Six Sisters Publishing
P.O. Box 254
Alamogordo, NM 88310

Library of Congress Control Number: 2002112423

ISBN 0-9724077-1-5

Printed in the United States of America

*Mama, around 1939, standing in front of our beautiful
white mantel at 5958 Plymouth Avenue.*

To My Mother

Mere words, be they English or Serbian,
could never describe the feelings in my heart
for Moda Trifunov Petrov, so I shall not try.

Contents

In Appreciation

Hours and hours and months and months of her life were give tirelessly by my precious daughter, Christina Williams, to place my memories where they would be read and remembered, and perhaps become an inspiration to others to record their life stories. May God bless her with good health and peace of mind for the rest of her sojourn on planet earth.

I am also very grateful to my brothers and sisters for giving me their thoughts and remembrances, often helping to jolt my memory where needed.

Angela Hamingson

Claude Petrov

Ruby Thomas

Dorothy Blades

Jimmy Petrov

Stella Gault

Bee Bee Davis

Introduction

*M*y story is a simple one. It began with the great rush of immigrants from Eastern Europe to America at the turn of the century. Many of these immigrants became the backbone of our great country. They were hard-working, grateful people who immediately set their sights on learning English and becoming a part of everything American. Many had large families, and they taught their children Christian living and love of country.

Two Serbian peasant families emigrated from the same province in Yugoslavia to Regina, Saskatchewan, in Canada within seven years of each other. Although they didn't know each other in the old country, the son from one family and the daughter from the other met in Canada and married. Those were my parents, Arthur Petrov and Moda Trifunov. When I was five, our family moved to the wonderful United States of America where Papa and Mama spent the rest of their lives raising their eight children.

As I grew older, I came to appreciate what my parents and their families went through to make a better life for themselves and their descendants. I respected Mama and Papa for their perseverance and commitment to each other and to us kids. Family was everything to them, and that's the way I am today.

My brothers and sisters and I each have our own memories from the days we lived at 2943 Chouteau Avenue in St. Louis during the twenties. We have always had lots of fun talking about people and events from those days, and many of my brothers' and sisters' recollections are scattered throughout this book.

On Chouteau Avenue we all learned English, but we spoke some Serbian too. I have included in this remembrance some of the Serbian words we used. They are written as I remember pronouncing them, not in their proper form or with correct spelling.

During the time I was writing this book, my darling brother Jimmy died in May 1999. Then in October 2001 my oldest sister Angie, who gave up her childhood to take care of us, went on to her reward. My generation is passing away. It is my greatest hope that our dreams and our values will be remembered and our heritage preserved through stories like this.

Here is my story.

Today is September 8, 2002.

Yesterday was September 8, 1921.

Chapter One

In the Beginning

"Everybody, stop what you're doing and come downstairs!" The urgency of Claude's little voice caught Mama and Papa's attention. Angie and I too stopped racing up and down the back porch stairs, and even baby Jimmy quit crying for a moment.

"Come look at what I saw on the street! Come right away!" He added, running back down the front stairs to the street. What could five-year-old Claude have seen that had him so excited? We were just moving into this simple two-room flat at 2943 Chouteau Avenue. But we had lived in the big city of St. Louis over a year, and we had seen many new things.

Papa and Mama quickly set down the bed frame they were putting together. Mama grabbed Jimmy, and she and Papa stepped over the piles of clothes they were unbundling and started down the front stairs. Angie and I ran after them down the long flight of wooden steps painted brown. Ruby and Dorothy toddled behind us. When we all arrived in the street, we stood there for a few seconds, blinking in the sun and looking around for whatever it was that had Claude so wound up.

At once Claude pointed down the sidewalk and said, "See, it looks just like me—and I'm sure it's a boy—but it's all black!"

Sure enough, there was a boy about five years old—and yes, he was all black! Seeing an entire family staring at him so intently, the boy did what anyone else in his position would have done: he picked up a rock and threw it at us!

None of us kids had ever seen a black person before—or a colored person, as everyone said then. As we stood there on the street, little did we know that this was only the first of many new experiences our poor immigrant family would have at 2943 Chouteau Avenue—and that this would be the place where my brothers and sisters and I would have our most joyous childhood adventures.

Just over a year earlier we had been living on a wheat farm in Canada. That's where my parents met and married—in Regina, Saskatchewan—and that's where they started our family. My story begins there.

To most people, Papa and Mama were just two out of the millions of immigrants who came to the New World from Europe around the turn of the century. But to my sisters and brothers, Papa and Mama were the ones who risked all they had and sacrificed their personal dreams to lead us out of a life of poverty and give us the wonderful opportunity of becoming Americans.

Papa and Mama were of Serbian descent. They were both born in tiny villages in Banat province, an area of Eastern Europe that belonged to Austria-Hungary when Papa and Mama lived there, but later became part of Yugoslavia. Papa and Mama didn't know each other in the old country, even though they grew up in towns less than twenty miles apart. In the early 1900s their families emigrated to Regina, Saskatchewan in Canada.

Papa's family homesteaded one hundred and sixty acres south of Regina near Avonlea. Later, when Papa came of age to need a wife, his family's farm was established enough to make Papa a good catch. Mama's parents heard about Papa and urged Mama to marry him, but Mama wasn't ready to marry. She liked another boy, and she didn't want to marry Papa. Her mother finally convinced her, though, that marrying Papa was a good decision, so Mama went along with it.

Papa and Mama on their wedding day, with
Mama's brother Duke and Papa's sister Dorothy.

"This is the way it went when we came to Canada," Mama explained in her broken English. "There was lots of boys, but very few girls. And all the boys would like to get married, but there wasn't enough girls to go around. So my cousin lived on a farm, and she thought that I should marry Artur, that they should bring him into town—we never got introduced or nothing. They just brought him into town, with his father and mother they came, and they asked for me to marry him. That's the way they do in Europe, and that was still European way. They didn't know no different, see. So, that's the first time we met. And a couple months later, we got married."

After the wedding Mama moved in with Papa's family on their farm. That was the European way, Mama said—especially when your in-laws had only one son. Then it was a disgrace not to live with them, whether you liked it or not. I'm not so sure Mama liked it.

"Then we had children," Mama said later, adding in her funny English, "We had babies after the babies."

My oldest sister Angeline came first. Angie always had a great big smile, and her eyes twinkled. She was the most happy-go-lucky child. To Angie, life was great. She didn't worry about things. Sixteen months later I was born. Mama and Papa named me Militza after Mama's mother, but they called me Millie.

Within a year and a half a son, Vladimir, came along. He was called Vlada until he started school, then he was called Claude. That's what we call him now. Papa was proud when Claude was born. When we were all older, Papa laughed and said, "I wanted to have a lot of boys, but I had a lot of girls!" We girls were glad too to have a brother.

Less than two years after Claude was born, Mama and Papa had a daughter, Ruby. Ruby was a beautiful baby with big brown eyes. Mama and Papa called her Lyuba. She was sweet and obedient, and she easily became Papa's favorite. After a little more than a year, Dorothy arrived. So the first five of us were born in Canada. Dorothy was pretty, giving Ruby some competition. She loved to play, and she always looked at the bright side of things. Dorothy accepted whatever life gave her without being sad.

Papa farmed in Canada, but he also tinkered with his inventions. He was always trying to come up with new and better ways of doing things. For quite a while he had been working on a pump, a perpetual motion mechanism that involved weights. When the weights were released, water was automatically pushed up the tap. When the weights were pulled up, the water flow shut off. He finally perfected Petrov's Magic Pump and had it patented in Canada. Some American lawyers contacted him about it, telling him that if he came to the United States, they'd make him a lot of money.

Papa must have manufactured a few Magic Pumps because Claude still has one, as

A Memory from Claude

When I was just a few months old and very sick, my mother was holding me in her arms, and I was barely breathing. Mother's friend looked at me, then said to Mom, "He's dead. You might as well call the undertaker." Mama responded by loudly calling my name: "Vlada!" I don't know whether she called me back from the dead or what, but I woke up suddenly. This apparently saved me from death, since I'm still alive today, over eighty years later!

A Memory from Ruby

Papa delivered me because they were living on the farm then. He didn't get all the afterbirth out, and Mama almost died from the infection. When Papa went to Regina to record my birth, he gave my name as Ljubitsa, after his mother. The clerk said, "You can't give her a Serbian name." So he picked out "Ruby" because it sounded enough like Ljubitsa.

well as a stock certificate to the pump company. Papa's pump wasn't so magic after all, and his venture failed. But in the curious way things happen, Petrov's Magic Pump actually led to something even greater than riches: our move to America.

Papa decided to visit St. Louis in January 1920. He picked St. Louis because some of

A Memory from Dorothy

One day after I grew up, I asked Mother what day I was born on. "Sunday," she said right away. "I remember it very vividly." They were going to church in a wagon. Mother was carrying me, and she said, "Oh, Artur, I think the baby's coming." So they stopped at a friend's house on the way. This lady said, "Oh, no, no, no! I don't want you to have the baby here. You leave the kids with me and go home and have your baby."

So Mother left the kids with her and went back home. When they got home, Papa laid newspapers on the floor and put a sheet over them. Then Mother squatted down and had the baby, telling Papa what to do all the while she was having me. And then, as I came out, I was screaming, and Papa said, "Oh, Mama, this is a loud one!" And I've been talking ever since!

Mother told me that story after I had children. When I had my babies, the doctor said, "You don't have to suffer. Just tell me if you have a pain. I'll take care of it." After Mother told me how I was born and what she went through, I could never, ever, ever love her enough, and I wanted her to know it. She was probably out working in the fields two days later.

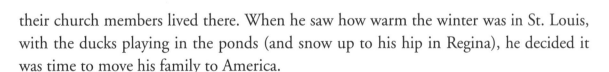

A Memory from Mama

My brother Duke wanted to go with us to the United States. Papa did the—I guess you call it visa—that's the permits we made cause we going to go the United States, you see. We paid the fees and everything, and we didn't have no trouble. But my brother thought he can just go with us, and he'll go in the bathroom and lock himself in while the border man goes though, see. And he put us in the trouble. So they took us all off, with five children, and Grandpa and Aunt Katherine. And put us up in a little town till they straighten up everything. They wouldn't let us go because he came with us, you see. I don't know how come that they didn't get a room for us or nothing. We slept on the floor in the police station—all of us on the floor. And what did they do with him? They sent him back. Next day, the train came, and we went on.

their church members lived there. When he saw how warm the winter was in St. Louis, with the ducks playing in the ponds (and snow up to his hip in Regina), he decided it was time to move his family to America.

On July 15, 1920, Papa, Mama, Angie, Ruby, Claude, Dorothy and I boarded the train in Regina and headed for our new life in America. Papa's father (we called him *Daka,* "Grandpa" in Serbian) and Papa's sister, our Aunt Katherine, came along too. I noticed the words "Soo Line" on the side of the train. I was proud that I could make out the letters since I was only five.

On the train we rode in our own compartment complete with a washstand, a white one. We never had anything like that on the farm, and we children admired it so! If people wanted to come in to our compartment, they had to knock. We felt as if we had our own little bitty house right there on the train—and that's where we stayed for the whole ride. I'm sure Papa was afraid to go to any other part of the train for fear it would cost more!

Someone had told Papa and Mama that food was expensive on the train, so we brought our own—mainly Mama's home-baked bread. To us kids the ride was like a picnic. We enjoyed it immensely, but whether the grown-ups did or not, I don't know. There was, of course, no air conditioning in those days, so we opened the windows. Soot flew in our faces and got on our clothes, but we loved every minute of it.

When the time came to get off the train in St. Louis, the porter knocked on the door, came in and started to brush off Papa's coat. But Daka told Papa quietly in Serbian, "Don't let him do anything for you. Someone told me they expect money for this." Papa immediately walked away. That poor porter probably wondered what we immigrant people were doing. I'm sure he never got a tip from us, as Papa and Daka had never heard of tipping.

Here is a picture of Papa taken in St. Louis in 1920, right after we came to America.

When we got off the train, Papa and Daka led the way. Claude got his foot caught in the rails, and Daka yelled at him. Angie, Ruby and I came running along next. Papa's sister, Katherine, followed behind with Mama, who had baby Dorothy in her arms. Mama always seemed to have a baby to carry.

Mama says that the summer of 1920 was the hottest summer ever in St. Louis. Maybe it seemed that way to her since she was accustomed to Canadian weather. All nine of us crowded into a small house that some friends from the church lived in. We stayed with them for a couple of weeks until Papa and Mama rented a flat on Ferry Street.

How excited I was to go to kindergarten! I had never been to school before. Clay School was high up on a hill, and we had to climb lots of steps to get to the top. The chairs and the tables were slick, varnished blonde wood. I had never seen furniture made of light wood before, as all the furniture we ever had was a deep brown color. My memories of that school are pretty little colored papers and crayons and small scissors and taking naps on the floor on a pad. Angie and I both felt so lucky to go to a school that had such beautiful furniture and beautiful paper. We liked it, and we wanted to stay there forever.

But after about six months we moved to a flat at 710 Seventh Street to be closer to a secondhand clothing business Papa had bought. We lived downstairs, and Aunt Katherine and Daka lived upstairs. Several times we heard Aunt Katherine scream when Daka beat her. We didn't like him for that. Angie remembers that Mama caught and killed rats at night at that apartment. They were as big as cats, she says. Mama fended them off from baby Dorothy.

Milan Petrov, Papa's father, whom we called Daka, which was our Serbian word for "Grandpa."

Daka was the boss in the family. He ordered Papa around and Mama too. Many foreigners believed that the oldest male was the one in charge. Daka worked the whole time he lived with us, but he never contributed any money to the household. He saved every penny he made so he could go back to Yugoslavia. He expected Papa and Mama to provide for him. When we moved the next time, Daka and Katherine got their own apartment. Then Daka visited us in our crowded two-room flat and bragged about all the food that he and Katherine had, while Papa and Mama had little or nothing to feed us with. But they didn't dare ask Daka for anything. That just wasn't done. A few years later, Daka did move back to Yugoslavia, and Katherine stayed in St. Louis.

After a while Papa got acquainted with some man "with high ideas," as Mama said, and he convinced Papa to move his secondhand clothing business to Broadway, where the rent was forty dollars a month instead of fifteen. Well, the store went broke, the

∽∽∽

A Memory from Jimmy

My birth certificate gives the midwife's name and my dad's occupation: "peddler." My name was spelled J-i-m-y. When I joined the Navy during World War II, I had to take Dad to the court house with me to get the "y" knocked off to make my name Jim.

Pop used to tell me that since I was born in the United States, I was going to be president. So when we went to kindergarten, and everybody had to say what they were going to be when they grew up, I said I was going to be president. Some of the other kids made fun of me and we got into a fight. That was my first fight.

∽∽∽

friend disappeared, and Papa was left owing a fifty-dollar note that he had signed, but had never told Mama about. Soon after that, Mama had to start working.

Jimmy was born on Seventh Street less than a year after we arrived in America. Papa was proud to have his first United States citizen— and a boy at that! Claude remembers Papa bragging that Jimmy was the only one in our family who could be president of the United States because he was the only one born in America. What an adorable little boy he was! Jimmy was always a happy kid and fun to be around.

Just before Jimmy was born all of us kids got scarlet fever. According to Mama, Angie had it so bad "she was out of her head." When one of us got sick, we all came down with it. We had every sickness there was. Being poor Serbians, we didn't want to miss out on anything, I guess!

The health department put a sign on our door saying there was scarlet fever in the house. At age six I didn't know what a quarantine was, but I did know our sickness was something bad. That sign told people not to come into the house or they might get sick too.

The shades had to be pulled down during the day so the light wouldn't hurt our eyes. All we could do was lie there and talk to each other. Some of the other kids on the block were jealous because we got to stay home from school. We were cooped up for six weeks—and all that time Mama was pregnant with Jimmy! At last someone from the health department came to check us out. They told Mama we were well enough to get up, and they removed the quarantine sign from our door.

In the fall of 1921 Papa decided that his secondhand clothes would sell better in a neighborhood to the west. Since people lived above their businesses in those days, that meant another move. So once more we packed all our belongings in sheets, and all eight of us—

Papa and Mama in March 1921. Mama was taller than Papa. She always wore that cap she crocheted—the one with the ribbon woven through the edge so she could tie the cap tightly onto her head.

Mama, Papa, Angie, me, Claude, Ruby, Dorothy and baby Jimmy—moved into my beloved 2943 Chouteau Avenue, where Claude saw the little boy.

Mama didn't want to move to Chouteau Avenue. She said it was in a bad neighborhood, the worst place we could live. Her memories from 2943 Chouteau Avenue were sad and harsh. No wonder—she worked like a horse, struggled for every penny, took care of all us children and became pregnant yet again, cooked and cleaned and baked and missed a lot of sleep.

But for me, 2943 Chouteau Avenue was the best place we ever lived. On Chouteau Avenue we kids had the most childhood fun. We laughed a lot and played as much as we could. And though we were poor and we knew we were poor, everybody else was poor too. So none of that dampened our childhood spirits!

Our building was red brick, and it had three storefronts, with a flat above each. Ours was the middle flat. When we first moved there, Papa opened his secondhand clothing

The only photograph we have of 2943 Chouteau Avenue, taken in the sixties when Stella (on the left) and Dorothy went to see our old home. It has since been torn down. We lived in the middle upstairs flat.

store right below us. When his store closed up, which happened quickly, a confectionery moved in.

The streetcar tracks ran through the middle of Chouteau Avenue, but the clatter of the streetcars didn't bother us because it was constant. A red brick sidewalk ran along Chouteau Avenue in front of our house. Two white stone steps led up to our door, which opened onto a flight of wooden steps painted brown. Each step creaked and groaned as if wondering how much longer it had to bear the burden of humans and their worldly baggage.

At the top of the stairs was our door. It opened into the kitchen. Next to the kitchen was the front room, which doubled as our bedroom—one bedroom for all eight of us. Those two rooms plus the back porch would be our home for the next seven years.

We had a chiffonier in the front room (they call it an armoire today). Mama's church clothes and Papa's suit hung in there. Papa and Mama slept in a white iron bed, and we kids liked to stick our heads through the iron designs. I think the bed was really brass that Papa painted white. In those days people either painted everything white or they varnished it.

Papa slept on the side next to the wall and Mama didn't because she had to get up more often, as mothers do. Papa—oh, could we hear him during the night, always hacking and spitting. He coughed up a lot of stuff, which he just spit into the corner of

the room, where it piled up until the end of the week. Mama always scolded him, "Artur" (that's how Mama pronounced Papa's name), "why do you do that in the house? Go outside and spit!" But Papa paid no attention to her.

The worst of it was that Angie and I had to scrub up that pile in the corner of the room when we scrubbed the front room floor every week. Oh, how we hated that! We used rags that we rinsed in the scrub bucket. Then Mama had to wash those rags out.

In the back yard of 2943 Chouteau Avenue soon after we moved in. Claude is standing with Papa. My hand is on Dorothy's head. Angie is standing next to Mama, who is holding Jimmy. Ruby is at Mama's feet.

Angie and I and Ruby and Dorothy slept sideways in a big bed under a *dushek* filled with feathers. The foot of our bed touched the foot of Papa and Mama's bed. They suffered through our fights and our frolic. Sometimes we laughed until we were scolded and spanked and told to go to sleep, and sometimes we fought. We always talked or told stories under the *dushek*. It was hard to keep us quiet because we were so fun-loving.

We didn't think it was a hardship, all of us sleeping sideways in one bed. Most of our friends slept that way. We were happy all the time, except when I cried of course, but that was only me. I cried a lot. I don't know why. It must have been because I didn't think anybody knew what I was thinking. And I always cried if Mama didn't come home on time. I was afraid she would never come home again.

Every time Mama or Papa found me crying they scolded me and sometimes they gave me a little spank on the butt. I remember Mama asking me impatiently, *"Zashto plachish, Militza?"* I couldn't answer. I didn't know why I was crying. Sometimes I did know why, but I didn't want to say. Many things made me melancholy then. I guess I did

A Memory from Angie

If the children did anything wrong on Sunday, and Millie thought it was a sin, she would cry and cry the whole day. She was sure the Lord was going to punish them and send them to hell. I think that years ago the Apostolic Church thought that playing ball on Sunday was a sin. And Jim or Claude would play ball on Sunday— something that today would be thought of as relaxation with your family. But Millicent cried for them. Millicent grieved for everyone. She suffered and hurt for everyone's mistakes. She loved her family. I don't think she was aware that she was putting all that burden on herself. She was sad more than she was happy.

A Memory from Dorothy

Everything was either a tragedy or a wonderful thing with Millicent. If she had a sad love affair, it was tragedy. If something good happened, it was wonderful. There was no in between. Millicent was either way up, or way down. If she was ill, she was deathly ill. Millicent was very dramatic.

more thinking than the other kids, and too much thinking sometimes makes a child sad.

When I was nine, I heard "The Prisoner's Song" on the radio at a friend's home. The haunting melody and the lonely words captivated me. "Oh, I wish I had someone to love me, someone to call me their own." Then when I heard, "With the cold prison bars all around me, and my head on a pillow of stone," I ran home and crawled under the bed and cried for the prisoners who didn't have a soft pillow like mine at night. I wondered why someone would even make a stone pillow, let alone force a prisoner to sleep on one!

When I wanted to cry in secret, I hid under our high bed. Everyone we knew had high beds. The iron springs weren't covered with cloth as they are today, and they were taller than today's box springs. Sometimes Mama took the mattress off so she could use her long brush to clean the springs, brushing away all the *pauchkina*s that the spiders wove. When she wasn't looking, we all jumped up and down on the wire springs. Of course, our feet got caught in between the wires, and we got cuts and bruises. But, oh, how we laughed! After all, we had to find something to have fun with. We didn't have all the ready-made toys and games that children have now.

The toys we did have we kept under the bed. But there must have been some space

A Memory from Claude

When Grandpa Daka lived in St. Louis, he thought I was a pretty good kid. When I was about seven or eight, he made something for me that was supposed to be a toy. He was very good at carving, and he carved little notches in a stick. Another stick went with it, so when you rubbed one stick across the other, it made the noise of going across the notches, like "Brrrrr." That was supposed to be entertaining, a good toy. Today, if you gave that to a kid, he'd laugh at you. It would not be entertaining at all.

*Ruby and Dorothy
in late 1921.*

left because we always ran under the bed to hide when we were about to be beaten. It was about the only place we could hide in the two rooms we had.

Jimmy and Claude slept together in a small white iron bed. When Ruby was about six, she got a terrible fever, and she was allowed to sleep in that little white iron bed all by herself. We all stood around and looked at her and felt sorry for her and talked to her a little, but she just lay there and moaned. Of course, Papa was very worried because Ruby was his favorite. Ruby was always such a good little baby and a good little girl. She didn't cry much. She was so obedient and so sweet and she never asked for anything. She was a perfect child. I guess that's why Papa loved her so much. Besides, she was beautiful. She had great big gorgeous eyes.

Mama told Papa to rush out and buy a little bottle of milk, a half-pint. We hardly ever had milk to drink because it was too expensive. If we did have milk, it was only for the baby. But Ruby got to drink that milk since she was sick. We all stood around and watched her drink it. We wished we were sick so we could get some milk. Looking back, milk was probably the worst thing for her at that time.

"Papa, is Ruby going to die?" I asked anxiously.

"No, she's not going to die," he answered angrily. "No!" That was his determination. When Papa said she wasn't going to die, then we weren't so sad, because we believed our parents. But Papa went to get the doctor anyway to reassure himself that Ruby was not going to die.

When the doctor came, he told Papa and Mama that Ruby's appendix had burst and the poison was passing through her system. In those days a doctor was like a god, so when he said that's what the problem was, everybody believed him. But who knows? I wonder now if that's what really happened. The doctor gave Mama some powder.

Medicine was either liquid or powder, wrapped in a tiny piece of tissue paper. That's where the expression "Oh, go take a powder" came from. Mama opened the tissue paper, dropped the powder into a glass, stirred it and had Ruby drink it. It was really bitter, but Ruby never complained.

Ruby was in bed for another week or so with a high fever. Then she got well.

One night in the winter of 1922 we kids woke up because we heard hushed voices, and we could hear Mama moaning. The ceiling light was on in the room, and we peeked out from under our *dushek* to see Mrs. Domijan from next door standing next to our bed. When she saw that we were awake, she pushed our heads into our pillows and wouldn't let us see why the light was on and why people were talking. We heard Mama crying, and we thought she was sick, so we cried too. Soon we cried ourselves to sleep.

The next morning we all woke up to a nice warm room. It was wonderful not to have to wait for Papa to stoke the fire to make the cold go away. As we popped our heads up, we saw a small baby next to Mama in her bed. And that's how Stella came into our crowded world.

Stella was happy and didn't ask for a lot of attention. She turned out to be the down-to-earth child among us.

A Memory from Claude

We almost lost Ruby when she was a little girl. She got appendicitis, and they took her to a doctor, and the doctor apparently didn't diagnose it right. But her appendix broke in her bowels and she passed everything, instead of it breaking inside and her getting peritonitis.

In those days, if you got peritonitis, you died. Later they took Ruby to another doctor. They found out that the original doctor was a false doctor. He lived right near us, and many people went to him. But he had a false diploma. He was exposed, and he lost everything and went to jail.

Mama rocked Stella in a brown wooden rocker that stayed in the kitchen. Every year Papa varnished that rocker. In the spring men varnished everything in sight—chairs, wooden bed frames or any dark wood furniture—to make it all look real shiny. Then they put the furniture out in the sun to dry.

After Mama died in 1980, all of us brothers and sisters met at her house to decide who would get what. Mama had asked us to do that, and it was a good idea. I wanted

Millie, Dorothy, Claude, Ruby and Angie soon after we moved to America. When Papa looked at this picture, he said, "See how nice those chairs look?" He was proud of his varnish job.

that old brown rocker. I shipped it home and had it refinished. The man who worked on it told me, "I have never seen so many coats of varnish on a piece of furniture in my life." But that's what all the immigrants did then. They took real pride in everything being shiny.

Mama nursed Stella, of course, but when Mama went to work, we all took care of Stella and gave her milk in a glass bottle. When we didn't have milk, we gave her sugar water. We rocked Stella in that shiny brown rocker, and sometimes we fed her a bottle of sugared tea so she wouldn't cry while Mama was working around the house cooking, baking bread or washing clothes. (Little did we realize then that the tea would keep the babies awake rather than let them sleep!) When Stella started teething, Mama rubbed a metal spoon on her gums to help her tiny teeth break through.

After Stella came along, we needed more beds. So Papa brought home a brown davenette. It opened up into a bed at night so Jimmy and Claude could sleep in it. We were so thrilled that we had a davenette because other people had one and we wanted one too. It made our bedroom look like other people's front rooms!

When we got the davenette we all crowded around to watch Papa open it into a bed. We thought it was magic, the way it opened and closed. Jimmy wanted to try opening it, so Papa let him lift it up once and turn it into a bed. But the iron part closed on his little finger and cut some of it off. Drops of Jimmy's blood fell on the wooden floor. Mama was so upset that Jimmy was hurt! She washed off his finger and wrapped a clean white rag around it. Oh, did Jimmy cry! Years later Jimmy showed me

A Memory from Ruby

Jimmy was darling. He was a cute little boy with blonde hair—almost a white blonde up until he was four years old. He had the cutest smile. We adored that little guy—all of us girls. We just loved him. He was so happy-go-lucky.

the scar that was still on his little finger. Dorothy says Papa beat me for my part in the tragedy, but I don't remember that. Funny, what we remember and what we don't.

While the rest of us had thick, almost black gypsy hair, Jimmy had blonde hair when he was a young boy. Papa always cut our hair, and he gave all of us Buster Brown haircuts. I guess that was the easiest for him. At some point Papa decided Jimmy was too old for a Buster Brown haircut, so he gave Jimmy a regular haircut instead. Oh, Mama almost cried. She complained that he no longer looked like her little baby boy. Instead he looked like a *boy* boy.

Jimmy was Mama's favorite. Even though she said she didn't have any favorites, we all knew that she loved Jimmy the most. We used to tease her about it. She let Jimmy get by with things that we never got by with. But somehow it never bothered us. We weren't angry or jealous. We just accepted it.

We didn't have electric lights then, even though the stores on the block did. The ceiling light in our room was a single gas mantle. Papa stood on a chair and took the glass off to light it. When the mantle needed replacing, we had to live in the dark until Papa and Mama saved enough money to buy another one.

One day Mama sent me to the store to buy a mantle for the gas lamp. On the way home I opened the box and took the mantle out. I had always wanted to touch one because they looked so soft and pretty. My finger had barely touched it when it disintegrated. We would have another dark night! Tears sprang out of my eyes because I knew I'd get it when I got home, and I was right. Papa beat me. "Why did you do that? Why did you touch it?" We weren't supposed to be curious, I guess.

Our front room had two tall windows that opened onto the street. In the summertime if it was a little cooler in the mornings, Mama slid the windows up to let the cool air in. When the sun came out, she closed the windows and pulled down the shades.

Everyone just took the heat for granted. Many a time in the summer we couldn't sleep because it was so hot. If we got too hot, we just fanned ourselves. Every store and funeral parlor gave away cardboard fans with advertisements on them. If one of us got sick, the others fanned her with a cardboard fan. Now and then I saw a fan that somebody actually bought, a fancy one, but I knew we could never have one of those.

Every spring we did spring cleaning, which included washing all our lace curtains. Everyone washed their curtains, then used a wooden curtain stretcher to dry them on. We put the stretcher together on the floor, then stood it up. It was as wide and long as the curtain—really large. We must have borrowed one, because I don't have any idea where we would have kept a wooden frame that large. It had tiny nails driven in around the frame to act as hooks.

When Mama washed the curtains, she put a lot of starch in the rinse water so the curtains could almost stand up by themselves when they were dry. Angie and I stretched each wet curtain across the frame, then we hooked the edges onto the nails all the way around. So many times we got our fingers caught on the nails, and they bled. Mama scolded us if we got blood on the curtains.

Sometimes Mama put the curtains out in the sun to dry, but then it was harder to bring them in because they were stiff as a board and we could hardly get them through the door! I don't know why everybody wanted them that stiff, but they did. After we hung those stiff lace curtains on the rods on the windows, they stayed there till next spring when we did it all over again.

We never washed the walls because the wallpaper would peel off if we did. Instead we bought wallpaper cleaner that came in a can. It had the consistency of putty, except that it didn't stick to our hands at all. We softened it by rolling it in our hands, then we used it like an eraser, rubbing it over every square inch of the wallpaper. Since everyone had coal stoves, the grime really built up on the walls. As we rubbed, all the black bits would fall to the floor, and we swept them up. Oh, the wallpaper would be so pretty after we cleaned it that we all wanted a chance to do it. "Look at this flower, how beautiful it is," we said as the

This was taken in the alley behind our house. Papa always lined us up by age to take a picture. Angie was the oldest, then Millie, Claude, Ruby, Dorothy, little blonde Jimmy and Stella with the doll. Dorothy always had that look on her face!

true colors came out again. If we had any of the cleaner left over after cleaning our wallpaper, we gave it to our neighbors so they could clean their wallpaper. Everybody cleaned their wallpaper every spring.

Papa and Mama were peasants, poor peasants, when they were children in

*A Memory
from Claude*

*Millie was sort of like the
general in our family. She really
took charge and led the rest of us.
If Millie said something, we did it.
She seemed more knowledgeable
about everything than the rest of
us. I don't know how come, but
she was. And Millie was the
leader of the four girls, even
when they were older.*

Yugoslavia. But they were clean people, and they taught us that being poor has nothing to do with being dirty. We were always clean and our house was always clean. Sweeping and cleaning and scrubbing were part of our daily lives. To Papa and Mama it were shameful to have children wear soiled clothes or to have a dirty house.

That's why it really bothered Mama to have so many roaches. As clean as Mama was, we still had roaches at 2943 Chouteau Avenue. Some of them could even fly. We hated how they crunched when we stepped on them, but we had to do it. None of us liked those big brown roaches, but Ruby screamed the most when they flew near her! The big brown roaches didn't stay only with us because the Domijans next door had them, and so did Mr. Caram's Greek restaurant downstairs.

Papa and Mama did the brunt of the work in the house, but we all had chores. Claude had to bring up the wood and the coal. That was a man's job, not a girl's job. I had chores such as sweeping and scrubbing, but my main job was bossing the other kids around—at least I thought so.

The back porch ran the length of all three flats, so Mama sat and talked to her neighbors there. Mama really had to watch baby Stella because when she was learning to walk she had a habit of running out the back door onto the back porch. Mama was always afraid Stella would tumble down the stairs into the back yard.

One day Mama decided to teach Stella a lesson so she wouldn't go near the stairs again. She held Stella tightly in her arms and stood at the top of the stairs and pretended to throw her down. Of course, Stella screamed. My heart jumped into my throat when I watched Mama do that. I was afraid she would drop Stella. Mama thought that would teach Stella never to go near the stairs again. Whether it worked or not I don't remember, but I don't think Stella ever fell down those stairs.

As for us older children, we loved to run down those stairs and play in the back yard. It was black dirt, with no grass at all, but it was our play land. There was always trash back there, junk that we played with. We created toys out of tin cans or pieces of cardboard. And stray cats were everywhere. I don't know where they came from, but there were always cats to play with. We certainly didn't feed them. I guess they ate the scraps from the Caram's Greek restaurant downstairs.

A couple of sheds stood in the back yard, plus the four toilets on one side. Each family had its own outhouse. No one would ever go to the other person's toilet. One toilet was ours, and it was up to us to bring the paper we needed there. For us that meant old newspapers and pages from catalogs. The toilet doors were slatted in such a way that we couldn't see in, but we could easily talk to whoever was inside.

Sometimes I was in the toilet when my best friend Katy came by.

"Where's Millie?"

"She's in the toilet," Claude replied.

So Katy came to the toilets and talked with me through the slats. It was just part of our play area.

The toilet seat itself was just a piece of wood with a hole cut in it. I never remember anyone cleaning out the toilets, so who knows whether it was done or not.

Dorothy was so brave. She had no fear of going outside to the toilet at night. Mama couldn't go to sleep when she knew Dorothy went down to the toilet because Dorothy stayed there for such a long time. Some nights Mama would find her just sitting on the toilet, rocking back and forth. When we found her like that, we told Mama, "Dorothy's moving again." That's what we called it—*moving*. But the rest of us weren't as courageous as Dorothy, so Mama sent Claude along to escort us at night.

If we had to use the toilet at night in the winter, we pulled out the *nokshir* from

Angie, Millie, Katy Borich, Ruby and Dorothy
in front of our toilets in the back yard. Isn't this
some background for a picture?

Ruby, Millie, Claude, Dorothy, Angie and
Jimmy on the wooden toys Papa made. I'm holding
an Easter basket from Buder Playground.

under the bed. The Watsons, who moved in next door after the Domijans left, called theirs a slop jar. If you had to go at night, you pulled out the *nokshir* and used it. We had to take turns emptying it in the morning. Ugh! No one liked that very much.

The Missouri Pacific roundhouse was right in back of us—in our back yard almost. Even though there was no fence between our yard and the railroad tracks, all the kids on the block stayed away from the tracks. The front of the roundhouse on Chouteau Avenue was red brick, and it seemed to extend for a long way. Of course, I was a little girl then and everything seemed bigger and longer, but it must have been at least a block long. The building was really rectangular, so I never could figure out why it was called a roundhouse!

After I learned to read, I could make out

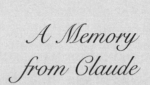

A Memory from Claude

The Missouri Pacific round-house had a bunch of windows, like in an old factory. Jim and I made our own slingshots out of inner tube rubber and a V-shaped fork from the tree. We got little metal pellets and broke those windows out. But they never did catch us.

the words people had painted on the red brick wall of the roundhouse. Once we read, "The girls in France wear tissue paper pants." That was five or six years after World War I ended. We didn't know what that meant, but all the little girls on the block sing-songed it anyway!

We children never tired of watching the trains slow down in our back yard as they pulled into the roundhouse. Some of the cars were heaped high with rich, black coal, and now and then a piece tumbled off and rolled into our yard. But that didn't mean it was ours, as all the kids on the block ran after it. Whoever grabbed it first got to take it home—that was the law of our poor neighborhood. After all, a big piece of coal in the stove could keep us warm for a whole evening.

At one end of our long back porch was a stairway leading up to the attic. The one attic window allowed some light in during the day—enough to go up there and read. It was a dusty place that smelled like dry wood—a real tinderbox if anybody had lit a match.

I took my little friends to the attic for a sewing club I started. We found rags here and there and cut them up and made things. I was the ringleader, and I felt so important to be able to show my little friends how to sew! We called the attic our clubhouse.

The attic was open above all three flats, so we could wander all over up there. Mrs. Caram, who lived next door to us, stored all kinds of clothes up there and other things she was going to take back to Greece to her less fortunate relatives in the old country. When she died they found two thousand silver dollars in a sock—money she was saving for her poor relatives. Her daughter, Bee Bee, told me that she told her husband about the money on her deathbed.

Papa and Mama had poor relatives in Yugoslavia too. They even mailed packages of clothes and medicine back to them later when they could afford it. Everyone who came from Europe always thought about their relatives in the old country. Papa and Mama often talked about how their relatives would be so surprised if they came to America and saw what we had here.

When Papa and Mama enjoyed good things in America—clothes and shelter and enough food to eat—they felt guilty. Their relatives back in Europe didn't have anything near what we had, even though we had next to nothing. In America we still had the one thing they didn't have: the opportunity to make something out of our nothing. That's why so many foreigners flocked to America. Our street was full of them.

Chapter Two

Immigrant Row

The 2900 block of Chouteau Avenue in the twenties was what I would call immigrant row. People lived above their shops—everyone except us. We lived above and didn't have a business below after Papa's secondhand clothing business folded.

Peanuts and George and Katy and Binky and little Dorothy Borich lived across the street from us. They were Croatian, and they had a saloon and restaurant right below them. Katy and I shared secrets. She was my best friend for a long time.

Once during Prohibition Katy's father went to jail for selling whiskey. When he came back, he had a big neighborhood celebration in their back yard. They roasted a lamb, and there was beer and root beer and strawberry soda for everyone. What a party they had!

When Katy first told me that they were going to roast a lamb, I couldn't imagine anyone doing that to a poor little lamb. All I could think of were the pictures of the little lambs in our books at school. The idea of roasting one appalled me!

But when we arrived at the celebration, the delicious smell of roast lamb permeated the air all around us. Then I thought maybe it was all right to roast a lamb after all. And when I tasted it, I was sure it was the right thing to do! For several years after that feast, though, I could close my eyes and see that poor little lamb carcass hanging over the fire.

At the party Mr. Borich showed everyone the wonderful portieres he had made in jail by tightly rolling up pieces of colored wallpaper to form makeshift beads, then stringing them on long strings. They hung in the doorway like a curtain. Katy's father was very proud of them, and everyone else admired them too.

One day Katy came over to play. We gathered tiny scraps of material from Mama's sewing basket, which sat on top of the treadle sewing machine in the kitchen next to the icebox. Chinese coins dangled from brightly colored threads on the end of the basket. I always looked at the coins with the square holes in the middle and wondered what the country was like that they came from, what the people there looked like and what they wore. Many years later I visited the Orient. By then there were no baskets like that, as most of them were in American antique shops!

"Let's go up to the attic so no one will bother us," I said. There we stitched the colorful scraps together to make potholders, all the while telling each other our innermost thoughts and feelings. Katy asked, "When you get married, Millie, who do you want to marry?" I didn't have to think about that much, for I had known the answer to that question for a long time.

"I want to marry a very smart man who likes to read books like me, and I want to live on top of a hill. And I want for him to be rich so I can eat anything I want forever—even bananas!"

Katy then told me that she wanted to marry a man who had a good job, and she wanted to have children. So I said, "Katy, let's pray to God so we can have our wishes." So we bowed our heads and closed our eyes and prayed.

Katy eventually married a man she liked who had a good job, just as she wanted. And in 1947, when I was thirty-one, I married a man who fit the description I gave Katy: a college-educated man who read books. And now I live in a house on a hill and I can afford bananas!

Katy and I met in the attic often and talked and talked as we sewed, planning our futures and sharing our hopes and dreams. Eventually we finished the potholders and gave them to our mothers. We were so proud that we knew how to make something. Even today I love that feeling of accomplishment I get when I finish something.

But one day Katy's mother died, and Katy and Binky and little Dorothy and George and Peanuts were left alone with their father. Katy's father told her that she couldn't go to school anymore because she had to stay home and cook and wash and iron and sweep. Katy was twelve, and I was sad.

Across the street near the end of the block was Mr. Moyer's blacksmith shop. He was a big strong man with a big strong voice. When we kids walked by, we looked in to see him in his long, dark blue apron, hammering hot iron pieces into horseshoes and holding them over a fire. He made horseshoes for the horses that pulled the carts for the iceman and the ragman and the man who sold vegetables.

All the little girls on the block knew that Mr. Moyer would make a ring for you from a horseshoe nail. So we stood at the side of his shop until he finished waiting on a customer. Then he came over to us and said in his big loud voice, "So, you girls want some rings, eh?" He strode over to his hot red fire and hammered the rings from horseshoe nails. As he gave each of us a ring, he felt us "down there." We didn't like it, of course, but it was only for a moment. Then we ran home with our precious rings. We told no one what he did. We just exclaimed to our parents, "Mr. Moyer made me a horseshoe ring!" That was the most important news to us anyway.

Mr. Bumstead's clothing and dry goods store was in the middle of the block on our

*A Memory
from Claude*

*Apparently, the guy who
wrote Dagwood Bumstead in
the comics was a brother of a
shoe buyer at Famous-Barr.
We knew him. He patterned
Blondie after a young lady
who worked in Bumstead's
Dry Goods store right on
our street—right on
Chouteau Avenue!*

side of the street, and we always peered into the window when we walked by. The little girls' dresses were so beautiful, with lace and satin ribbons in so many colors. But we knew those were for rich people—not us. Still, we loved to dream about wearing them.

Once when Angie and I were going to be in a race at the Chouteau School picnic, Mama said, "You both need new socks to go with those dresses, so let's walk down to Bumstead's." I was ecstatic that I was getting a new pair of socks! When we got to Bumstead's, we gazed at all the beautiful clothes and dresses. Then we looked at the socks, and Mama asked Mr. Bumstead how much they were. He mentioned a price that I didn't hear, and Mama replied, "Oh no, I don't have that much money."

Mr. Bumstead thought a moment, then suggested, "Well, come over here to the window. Here's a pair of orange socks that are faded from being in the sun." One sock was a pale yellow and the other one was still orange. "You can have these for twenty cents." That was still a lot of money for Mama, but she bought them anyway. Oh, was I thrilled and proud! Mama also bought Angie some new red socks because her dress was red silk. I don't remember what color my dress was, though, because the only thing that stands out in my mind was my fabulous socks!

Our socks were very shiny rayon, which was quite fashionable then. They were a little bit thick, and mine came up to just below my knees. Was I proud when I wore them with my dress at the Chouteau School picnic! It was wonderful. Angie and I felt positively *rich* when we wore our new socks.

Policeman walked their beats then, and our neighborhood policeman was Officer Callahan. Once when one of us kids kept wetting the bed long after we grew old enough to stop, Papa took the offending child to Officer Callahan and explained the problem.

Officer Callahan said, quite seriously, "Arthur, the next time your child wets the bed, you bring the little one to me and I'll put the kid in jail!" Papa and the officer winked at each other. Well, it worked. That was the last time Mama had to change wet sheets!

The Palazzolos lived four doors down from us, and they operated a fruit and vegetable store. When Mrs. Palazzolo had spoiled peaches that she couldn't sell, she sent her sons over with them. When we kids spotted the boys walking up the alley with bushels full of peaches, we yelled excitedly to Mama. She came out and looked over the porch. "Bring them up," she told them. Mama was glad to get them. She just cut out the bad parts and made jelly with them or put them up in jars. Sometimes Mama accepted the peaches and other food in exchange for washing and ironing for Mrs. Palazzolo.

My, the peaches were delicious in those days! They were ripe and we could eat them right away. Today they're hard as rocks, and even if you set them out for a week, they get rotten before they get ripe.

Mrs. Palazzolo gave Mama spoiled tomatoes too. We all helped carry the tomatoes home. Mama

At the Chouteau School picnic in 1927. I am on the left with my shiny rayon socks. Angie has on a red silk dress that someone gave her and her new socks. Don't we look thrilled?

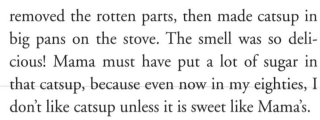

A Memory from Claude

The Palazzolos owned a fruit market in the middle of the block on our side. They made their own liquor there during Prohibition and sold a lot of it. Gus Palazzolo's uncle used to come to our back yard and kill rats. There was one place where the rats stuck their noses out of a hole in the building, and he was so good with that gun, he could hit them with just a little bit of their bodies sticking out.

removed the rotten parts, then made catsup in big pans on the stove. The smell was so delicious! Mama must have put a lot of sugar in that catsup, because even now in my eighties, I don't like catsup unless it is sweet like Mama's.

We all stood around and watched as Mama carefully poured the catsup into the bottles through a tin funnel, then handed the full bottles to Papa. He had a magic iron machine that capped the bottles with the prettiest gold-colored caps we ever saw. Once we had to wait two days to put the catsup in those bottles because there was no money to buy caps. But when the bottles of delicious catsup were capped, we put them under the bed until we used them. It was certainly getting crowded under our bed!

The Bogdanoviches ran a little food market on our block. When we went in, Mr. Bogdanovich was behind the counter. We asked for what we wanted, and he went through the store, gathering the items for us. We stood in front of the counter waiting. It wasn't like the help-yourself supermarkets of today. A lot of people had running tabs there, and Mr. Bogdanovich added onto their tabs whenever they came in to buy something. When payday came, people paid some on their bills. Store owners trusted all the immigrant families because they knew we would pay someday. Most of us had running bills in all the stores.

Once Mama went to work on a Saturday and left us ten cents for lunch to buy some bologna to eat with our bread. We walked across the street to Mr. Bogdanovich's market and bought a pound of butter instead, then we made toast in the oven. Boy, did we think we were in heaven, eating real butter instead of lard! It was so delicious. It was such a treat that many of my sisters remember it to this day.

The Domijans, a Croatian family, lived in the flat next to us. Papa and Mama could speak in Serbian with them pretty well, but I couldn't make out some of their words. We said *leba* for bread, and they said *kruha*. That difference made a big impression on me because bread was such an important part of our lives. Everything we ate revolved around bread, and often all we had was bread.

Once when Papa worked repairing dolls at Famous-Barr Department Store, he brought home some broken roly-poly clowns that couldn't be fixed. He glued and painted them as best he could and gave them to us. It was fun to put the clowns on the floor and tilt them and watch as they rolled from side to side but never fell over because they had round bottoms! One of the clowns was green like trees. I wanted him for myself, and Papa said yes, he could be mine. I played with him so much, and he made me laugh when I looked at him. At night I kept him under my bed. When I got up in the morning, I crawled out from under the *dushek* and looked under the bed to make sure he was still there. Sometimes I snatched him out and hid him under the *dushek* to warm him up till Mama called us to get out of bed.

A Memory from Claude

When we lived on Chouteau Avenue, we had a very heavy-set Irish policeman whose name was Callahan. Millie was at that age when she had just found out where babies come from. This fellow was pretty robust in his mid-section, pretty heavy—almost looked like he was pregnant. So she asked him, "Officer Callahan, when you have those police puppies, would you give me one?"

The Domijans had a daughter my age named Olga, and we played together. Once Olga was hit by a car as she was crossing our busy Chouteau Avenue. Because Olga was in an accident and even in the hospital for a while, Papa and Mama wanted to give her something. They decided to give her my green clown that was the color of trees. Olga had always liked my green clown and wished it was hers. I knew I should be kind to her because she was hurt, but I didn't want to give her my roly-poly clown. However, I had to do it, and when Olga took the clown from my hands and smiled, I ran into the front room and cried in the corner for a long time. I didn't like Olga anymore, and I wished they would move away. Soon after that they did.

When Olga Domijan and her family moved out of the flat next to ours, the Watsons moved in. They were a colored family. I don't remember who saw them first, but I do remember that the day they moved in, we didn't talk to them. The next evening there was a knock on our door. Mama answered, and Mrs. Watson was standing there with a pie in her hands. "Mrs. Petrov," she said politely, "I made this pie for you and your family." Mama thanked her and she brought the pie in. Then we all sat around and discussed whether we should eat it or not because it was made by a colored person.

"Well, they seem real nice even though they're colored people," Papa reasoned. As we talked about it, the aroma of the pie got the best of us, so we gobbled it up. From then on our families started talking to each other. It was very nice of Mrs. Watson to make the first gesture. We became very good friends after that. After we got better acquainted with the Watsons, Mama realized they were wonderful Christian people, and Papa liked them too.

Thelma Watson and I became good friends. We were the same age—about ten when they moved there in 1925. They were very clean people and we were very clean people. We took turns scrubbing the white stone steps on the street that led to our shared staircase.

Old Grandma Watson was so sweet. She sat and sang religious songs all day long as she rocked inside her house. We could hear her from the back porch we shared. Mrs. Watson and Mama often met and chatted on the back porch, and they borrowed sugar or flour from each other. Once they canned green peppers at the same time. Thelma and I gathered all the cores and pretended we were canning them too.

The Watsons had an undertaking parlor downstairs below their flat. Mama warned us to stay out of the way when a funeral was going on, so we were careful to do that. The back windows of their funeral parlor were painted black on the inside so people couldn't look in. But our curiosity about what went on in there got the best of us, so Thelma and I came up with a plan. She sneaked into the funeral parlor and scratched a tiny piece of the black paint off the window. Then we found some old wooden boxes and propped them up in the back yard below the window. When we stood on the boxes and looked in, we saw Thelma's father embalming a man. When I saw that dead man lying there, I was really scared and so was Thelma. We jumped off the boxes and ran. After that we never looked in again.

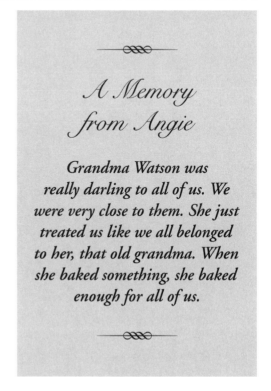

A Memory from Angie

Grandma Watson was really darling to all of us. We were very close to them. She just treated us like we all belonged to her, that old grandma. When she baked something, she baked enough for all of us.

We kids watched quite a few funerals, so we got the idea to have our own funeral. We found an old matchbox to use as a coffin. A dead cockroach, which was easy to find, served as our corpse. We ceremoniously laid him in the box. Then some of us carried the box, and the rest of us walked behind slowly, trying not to smile. We put our sad faces on, just like the people in the real funerals did.

Our procession moved along to the side of our building. There Claude dug a hole with a stick, and we placed our coffin into the hole and put dirt on top of it. Then we sang "Jesus Loves Me," and we tried to imitate one of the religious hymns Grandma Watson sang.

> *A Memory from Angie*
>
> *We sat on the bench in front of Caram's restaurant and counted the automobiles. Back then, they only made black cars and brown cars. Suddenly cars began to come in colors. So we sat out there and counted the cars that were in colors.*

I'm glad the Watsons lived next door to us because they were the first black people we met, and the Watsons were wonderful. We liked them, and we found out from knowing them that black people were no different from us.

The Carams lived on the other side of us, and they operated a Greek restaurant below their flat. Mrs. Caram was very kind to us. She brought us leftover food from the restaurant because she knew we had it hard and didn't always have enough to eat.

Claude remembers the Missouri Pacific railroad men going to Caram's to eat. They worked in the offices of the railroad building next door. Part of that building was a gymnasium, and the Missouri Pacific sponsored boxing matches there. One of our friends from across the street, Peanuts Borich, boxed there, and we went to watch him. He became a well-known boxer, and so did Tony Viviano, another boy who lived down the street.

Ruby and Dorothy played with Jimmy and Petie Caram. Once they found a piece of screen, so they decided to sift dirt through it, looking for treasures. From then on they often said, "Let's play *seya*-dirt," as they called their new game. They sifted dirt for hours. Sometimes they found a bottle cap or even a penny, but usually they settled for old nails and rocks.

Although Katy was my best friend, the Caram's daughter Bee Bee, who was three years older than me, was my idol. She was my movie star and the person I wanted to emulate. Bee Bee spoke good English and smiled all the time. She was so pretty. I felt I could never match up to her in looks, but I tried to copy everything else she did and

A Memory from Ruby

The Vivianos down the street had a kind of market and restaurant. Mrs. Viviano had a lot of kids. She did all the work while her husband ran the store and pretended like he was the big guy—a typical foreign situation. It was same with the Greek family next door to us. Mrs. Caram did all the cooking and cleaning and preparation of the food, and Mr. Caram would stand at the cash register and chin with all the railroad men.

We kids went into the Caram's restaurant freely. Mr. Caram liked all of us and he tolerated it. Mrs. Caram was too busy cooking back there to worry about it. I went in there once, and a customer was eating ice cream. He looked at down at me, and I must have looked up at him like, "Gee, I'd like to have some." So he gave me a spoonful of ice cream. If my mother had known that, she would have died. In fact, I think I got two spoonfuls from him, I must have looked so pitiful. I still remember to this day how rich and smooth that vanilla ice cream tasted.

said. Through all the things she showed me, I learned how much influence a person can have on a little girl.

When I was twelve, Bee Bee Caram was in high school. Her mother bought her all the latest clothes. Of course, Bee Bee had money—not much, but loads compared to us. She could always get money from her parents for anything she wanted. I can close my eyes now and see the beautiful silk dress she wore when short dresses that came up to the knee became popular. She wore beautiful silk clothes to school all the time.

When I walked down the street with Bee Bee I was so proud that I was with her and that she was my friend. Everybody looked at her because she was so pretty, and she was well-liked because she smiled so much and made everybody feel good. When Mama told

My best friend Bee Bee Caram.

me I couldn't go to high school because I had to work to help support the family so the other kids could go to school, I ran over and cried on Bee Bee's shoulder. I wanted to go to school so I could learn more. Bee Bee hugged me and said, "Don't cry, Mimsy. I'll teach you everything they teach me in high school."

Mrs. Caram's bedroom (which, like ours, doubled as a front room) had a beautiful large bed in it with a crocheted bedspread that came all the way down to the floor. Bee Bee and I often crawled under that bed, and there in our hideout she read and explained things to me. Most of the time we slid under the bed so her mother couldn't find her. Mrs. Caram would stand at the bottom of the stairs in the restaurant and call for Bee Bee in Greek, "Where are you, Bee Bee? I want you to come down and help me in the restaurant." Bee Bee just put her finger to her lips. We stayed quiet so she wouldn't find us.

Bee Bee and I sang the popular songs together, like "It's Three O'Clock in the Morning" and "It Ain't Gonna Rain No More." One day Bee Bee showed me pictures of the movie stars in a magazine. When I saw the picture of BeBe Daniels, I told Bee Bee that I thought she looked like her since she had the same short dark hair and beautiful eyes and always a smile like hers. I loved the picture of Clara Bow. The other movie stars were pretty too, but Clara Bow looked as if she did some of the things I would like to do! I thought Pola Negri looked as if she were always thinking of something she didn't want anyone else to know. They were all beautiful, and I looked up to them as though they were queens.

As we turned the pages of the movie star magazine, we came across a picture of a gorgeous man. "Who is this?" I asked excitedly.

"Rudolph Valentino," Bee Bee responded, proud that she knew.

"Oh, I never saw a man so beautiful," I declared. Later I saw him in *The Sheik* at the outdoor airdome, as they called it, on Chouteau Avenue and Jefferson. It cost a nickel to get in, but it just looked like somebody's back yard with a fence all around it. We sat on wooden benches with no backs and watched the movie on a big screen in front. A man played tunes on the piano to go with the story, because the movies

Bee Bee Caram, looking like the movie star BeBe Daniels.

were silent then, of course. As I watched, I was transported into the stories. I sat there not even realizing where I was till the movie was over. Claude and Angie had to shake me to rouse me to go home.

We saw cowboy and Indian movies there with Tom Mix. A funny woman, Zazu Pitts, was also one of my favorites to watch. And, of course, we laughed at Charlie Chaplin. In those days, they played serials—stories that continued from one Saturday to the next. But we didn't get to follow those much because we didn't have an extra nickel very often.

Two or three times Bee Bee came to the house and asked Mama if I could go with her for a streetcar ride. Mama agreed, so I dressed up because Bee Bee was always dressed up. I was so proud when we walked outside and waited for the streetcar together. When the streetcar pulled up, Bee Bee paid the five cents for each of us. As we rode along, she explained different things to me. It seems as though she was always educating me.

A Memory from Ruby

Millie was a little embarrassed about not having an education. But Bee Bee Caram was so good for her because she made Millie read books that Millie would have read in high school if she had gone. Bee Bee would say, "Oh, Millie, you've got to read Les Misérables." Bee Bee told her to read many of the classics, and Millie educated herself just from reading. Then I read everything that Millie read. We still send each other books.

We all thought lots of Bee Bee. Mama and Papa especially cared for her, and she cared for them. They must have really liked her because Mama and Papa later named my youngest sister, Bee Bee, after her!

When I graduated from the eighth grade in 1929, I wore a beautiful white dress—at least I thought it was beautiful. I was so excited on graduation day. We were all on the stage, and when they called my name, someone handed me a bouquet of flowers with a card that read, "With love, from Bee Bee." I felt like a princess. Never did I dream that I would ever receive a bouquet of flowers! I thought flowers were only for movie stars or rich people.

My graduating class included Glenmore McClurg, Arthur Fair, George Salami, Stephen Kruthouski, Floyd Sharp, Louise Shlivstien, Margaret Millier, Josephine Bordonaro, Bunny Gallagher, Marie Berjek, Ellen Chani, Marie Gafron and Pearl Manley.

By the time I graduated, we had moved to a different house in the same neighborhood. There, on June 13, 1931, one week after Bee Bee graduated from high school, Mama was called to the telephone. She came back crying. Bee Bee's mother had died unexpectedly as a result of a gallstone operation. Oh, it was so sad for all of us. We all cried and cried—so much so that Papa wouldn't let Mama go to the funeral because he said she would make a fool of herself crying.

We read in the obituary that Mrs. Caram's last name was really Caramsalidis. They must have done what many immi-grants did—shortened their name so it was more Americanized and easier to pronounce.

After the funeral Bee Bee came over and told me that her father was taking her and her two little brothers back to Greece. What a black day that was for me. Then they sold the restaurant to another Greek man and started packing to leave.

On the ninth of July we went to the railroad station to say good-bye to the Carams. Bee Bee gave me a stamp book full, a tennis outfit, her raincoat, her pink party dress and

Here I am (on the bottom right) at my eighth grade graduation in the schoolyard with some of my best friends. I am holding the bouquet Bee Bee Caram had given to me while I was on stage. The girl in the white hat was my good friend, Bunny Gallagher.

her green taffeta gown. She and I clung to each other and cried. "I'll never see you again," I moaned.

"I'll write to you, Mimsy," she assured me.

"I'll write you too," I said between sobs. I clung to her as if I would never see her again. We had to say good-bye for the last time. It was terrible.

A month after they arrived in Greece, we got a letter from Bee Bee addressed to Mama. We were so thrilled! She described everything there in Salonika, right outside of Athens. As soon as they arrived in Greece, Bee Bee was offered a job teaching English at the high school. Of course, she didn't have a teaching degree, but the fact that she came from America and was a graduate of an American high school meant a lot in that small town in Greece in 1931. She also wrote, "The people here think I'm cracked because I want to take a bath every day!"

Seeing Bee Bee again for the first time after almost fifty years.

Bee Bee continued to write us letters from Greece. When I started working, often I came home from work and Mama excitedly showed me an envelope and said, "This looks like it came from another country." Mama couldn't read English, but she could tell the envelope looked foreign. I took a look and exclaimed, "Yes, it did come from Bee Bee!" Everybody wanted me to read it right away. "No, after we eat supper and wash dishes, then I'll read it to everybody," I announced. So that's what we did.

A few months later Bee Bee wrote that her father had remarried! Two years later we got a letter edged in black. Everyone knew what that meant. There was even a popular song out in the twenties, "The Letter Edged in Black." As soon as the letter came, Mama said, "Oh, look, Millie, somebody must have died." Indeed, someone had. Bee Bee's father had passed away. I saved that letter and still have it today.

One day we opened a letter from Bee Bee and saw inside a picture of the man she married. By that time she was teaching English at the college, and he was a teacher there also. His name was Chris Koloyeroponlov. Her new last name was so long I could hardly fit it across the envelope. She enclosed a picture of herself in her wedding gown with Chris, standing outside, with ducks and chickens all around. We looked carefully into Bee Bee's face, and she looked very happy. Later they had two children—a girl and a boy.

Almost fifty years after Bee Bee and I said good-bye to each other at the train station, my sister Ruby and I traveled to Greece. My dream finally came true, and I saw Bee Bee again. I think I would have recognized her if she had been walking down the street in my town—she looked so much the same. Was I overjoyed to see her! It was as if we had just said good-bye on that day so many decades earlier. She was still so sweet and beautiful, and she still had that sparkling smile. She didn't have many wrinkles either, and I always attributed that to the fact that they use olive oil there. Sometimes they put it on their faces, and so do I!

When we visited her, Bee Bee's daughter, Victoria, was living with her. Of course, we talked and talked about our times together on Chouteau Avenue. She asked about everyone in the family. I reminded her how grateful I was to her that she introduced me to books. What a wonderful thing it was to see Bee Bee again!

Years later Victoria wrote to tell me that Bee Bee had become ill. It sounded as if she had Alzheimer's. She just lay in bed for years, with her daughter taking care of her. I mailed her items that I thought would help Victoria, and things that would make Bee Bee laugh. I even sent a cassette tape I made of all the popular songs from the late twenties that Bee Bee would remember, and her daughter played it for her.

Then in 1999 Bee Bee Caram Koloyeroponlov passed away—my wonderful friend who was such an inspiration to me.

Chapter Three

When We Get Rich…

One day in late spring Angie and I were walking home from school. As we turned the corner onto our street, we saw a big, red iron crane right in front of our building. It was holding a piano in its mouth, high up in the air. What in the world was going on?

Immediately we ran to our flat and looked up. We noticed that our upstairs front window had been removed. The large crane was pushing the grand piano sideways into our front room through the empty hole where the window had been!

All my friends on the block and their fathers and mothers stood around watching, as none of us had ever seen anything like that before. Running up the stairs as fast as we could, we arrived in the front room just in time to watch the piano come down slowly into the room. There was Papa, proudly directing the workmen. He told them he wanted the piano placed right in the middle of the room. Seeing us, his face brightened as he announced, "See, now we have a piano!"

Angie and I ran to press the beautiful white keys to hear the heavenly sounds they made. It was a square grand piano, a big beautiful one with carved legs, made out of dark wood that I know now is mahogany. We knew when we saw how shiny it was that Papa wouldn't have to varnish it each year as he did the wooden chairs, tables and chests we had.

The piano took up all the space that was left in our front room. I asked Papa where we were going to put the round wood stove in the wintertime, but he didn't pay any attention to my trivial question in the midst of such a grand event.

I saw Papa pay the workers five dollars. They put the window back into the empty space, took their crane and left. I was glad when the window was back in place because that was the window I ran to every day after school. Each time I heard a streetcar screeching to a stop I looked out to see if Mama was getting off. I knew I could never go without that window.

Papa couldn't wait to surprise Mama with the piano. We too couldn't wait till Mama arrived home to see this wonderful present! We ran down the stairs and waited outside impatiently, watching for her. Finally we caught a glimpse of her slowly stepping off a streetcar. She had been cleaning house all day for Mrs. Barreta, and she was a little stooped. But we knew she would perk up right away when she found out what we had in the front room! As soon as we saw her, we all screamed out, "Oh, there's a surprise for you! Papa's got a surprise for you. Come upstairs, we can't wait for you to see it!"

As we led her upstairs, she was kind of smiling, and we were almost bursting with excitement. Then as the door opened, she peeked into the front room. There stood Papa, smiling broadly. All of us kids said, "Look, Mama. We've got a piano now." As her eyes fell upon the piano, she groaned and clasped her hands together, looking up to the heavens.

"Eyou! Bozhe moya!" she exclaimed. "Oh, my God!" was all she could say. Mama's

face had a sad look on it, as if she were almost going to cry. The first thing Mama asked Papa was, "*Koliko ye koshtalo?*" She wanted to know how much money Papa had spent on this unnecessary luxury.

"Just five dollars," Papa told her proudly.

Then in Serbian she cried out to Papa, "You don't have a job, we don't have the money to pay our rent, the children need shoes—and you spent five dollars on a piano? We can't eat a piano!"

For a while Papa and Mama talked back and forth. Then Mama started crying. We kids were all quite upset because we thought Mama would be so happy. We thought it was terrible of her not to like the wonderful piano. As for Papa, his big smile was gone and his face went dark.

Suddenly Papa ran through the kitchen to the back porch and returned with the ax he used to chop wood when we found a piece too big to fit in the stove. He stood by the big beautiful piano and started hacking it into pieces. Every time Papa chopped off a piece, he grabbed it and ran to the back porch where he threw it down into the yard. He muttered in Serbian the whole time, but I didn't understand what he was saying.

We edged back until we were against the wall. I was sad because I already liked the big beautiful piano. It made me feel as if we weren't poor. But it was disappearing before our eyes, piece by piece. Soon all that was left was the large, gold-colored iron harp, and we rushed forward to touch the strings to hear the heavenly music once more. That golden harp was so heavy, but somehow Papa dragged it from the front room, through the kitchen and onto the porch. There he pushed it over into the back yard, breaking off part of the wooden railing.

We thought Papa was right and Mama was wrong to make him feel so bad about buying the piano that he had to chop it up. No one talked much that night. Mama just remarked in Serbian that she always had to do the practical thinking in the family.

We played with that golden harp that lay in the dirt in our back yard for a long time. We also had extra firewood that winter. And Papa and Mama never talked about the piano again.

Papa wanted us to have the wonderful things in life other people had, but we didn't have the money for them. That's because Papa never wanted to work for anybody. He always wanted to be the boss, so Mama had to do housework for other families to put food on the table. She told me later in life that before Papa and his family left Yugoslavia, someone there—maybe a fortuneteller—told him that when he went to the New World, he would become a very rich and important man. That prediction went to Papa's head, Mama told me, and he believed that somehow it would just happen. Years later he was still waiting to become rich, until one day he realized that the opportunity had passed.

Many poor peasants in Europe thought they would get rich in the New World. That's one reason Papa's family dreamed of moving here. In June 1903 their dream came true. Papa's parents, Milan and Ljubitza Petrov, sold their cow, their sow and their home in Farkaždin, Banat province, and booked passage for their family to Canada. My papa, Arthur Petrov, was twelve.

For ten dollars Papa's family homesteaded one hundred and sixty acres about forty-five miles south of Regina. As they rode their horse and wagon south, looking for their land, the road turned into a trail and the trail into prairie. Still they went on, driving through the knee-high prairie grass "never cut since God made the earth," as Papa said. They finally found the section marker that told them they had found their new home. Papa's mother, Ljubitza, cried, and his father, Milan, fell to his knees and thanked God.

At first they caught and ate the rabbits that were abundant on the prairie. Papa's mother made rabbit *paprikash* stew. Then she fried the rabbit, boiled it and even roasted it, trying to make it taste different. But for weeks all they had was rabbit, rabbit, rabbit.

The summer days of the north had eighteen hours of daylight, and that helped Milan and Papa work long hours to get their house built in a week. It was the only house in the area with a peaked roof and a dormer window. Then they purchased horses and a plow, and the farming began.

Papa's father had been a carpenter in the old country, moving the family from town to town, building flour mills and making coffins. Each time they moved, Papa went to a new school, sometimes in an area where a different language was spoken. Because of

Here I am on the farm near Avonlea. The house Daka
built is in the background on the left with the peaked roof.

When I was in Canada in 1967, I went with my cousin, Mike Stankov, and his wife, Florence, to the Canadian Archives in Regina to look up Daka's homestead papers. A nice man set us up with a screen and a knob to turn. I kept turning the knob and reading—then sure enough there it appeared: "Milan Petrov." I was so thrilled to see my grandpa's name in print. In 1903 he signed the homestead application in Cyrillic. When he claimed the homestead patent three years later in 1906, his livestock was listed as four horses, two cows and four pigs. And he signed it in English: Milan Petrov.

that, Papa learned several languages. When his family moved to Canada, Papa's ability to speak other languages helped him get work in Regina (even as a young boy) interpreting in court for people proving their homesteads.

At age sixteen Papa worked for a while breaking wild horses on the Alek Mowatt ranch about four miles west of their farm outside Regina. His sister Dorothy said that he used to come home with blood running out of his nose and ears, he took such a beating from the horses. But Papa loved it because he loved a challenge.

Mama's brother Mac standing on Papa's thresher.

When Papa was eighteen he passed the test to become a steam engineer. He was so proud of that steam engineer's license, which he needed in order to operate a steam thresher to harvest the wheat. He must have made some money doing that because within a year he bought a used threshing outfit and hired it out with a small crew. Then he purchased three hundred and twenty acres next to his father's farm. He did exceptionally well at his first big undertaking. It was only the first of many of Papa's entrepreneurial efforts—some successful, many unsuccessful.

Papa always looked for a more efficient way to do everyday work (maybe in order to get out of the work), and that's what led him to invent things. And he always believed wholeheartedly that each invention was his key to riches—even his very first one!

Soon after they arrived in Canada, Papa's father went to work for the Canadian Pacific Railroad as a section hand to earn thirty dollars a month until the crops came in. One day when Papa's father was away at the railroad for the week, Papa saw a horseless wagon driving down the road and "perceived an urge to make one." His father had

A Memory from Claude

Pop made a list of inventions that he wanted to follow up on. There were about ten items on it. One of them was a combination tea and coffee pot. Another was a collapsible oil barrel that would save shipping space on the way home. The other one was the thing that all inventors try to invent: perpetual motion.

A Memory from Stella

Pop had in mind to design a swimming suit made of rubber so that a person could swim and float—one that wouldn't let the swimmer sink.

A Memory from Jimmy

In Canada, Papa was the first one who taught them how to use straw instead of wood and coal to power the steam engines of the threshing machines. He taught them how to bundle up the straw and throw the bundles in the machines. So they used the straw they were going to throw away to power the machine.

bought some good lumber to build a kitchen cabinet with, and Papa decided to use it to make his wagon. He made the wheels and the body out of the lumber, then he had the blacksmith who sharpened their plowshares make two axels and a few other little parts, charging them to his father's account. In three days, with his sister's help and a can of red paint, Papa had built a miniature horseless wagon. He drove it by pushing a cross handle to and fro while sitting in the seat, and he steered it with his feet.

Papa's sister warned him that their father would be angry when he found out what happened to his lumber and when he got the bill from the blacksmith. He would have to work an extra week for the railroad to pay for it, she said. Coming to his senses, Papa hid the wagon in a haystack. But somehow, Papa's father found it. That brought four strokes with the cane, and Papa couldn't sit for a week. But Papa had the last word when he was burning some brush later that fall and that cane happened to be in the brush pile!

Papa remembers, "So for my first invention I got a good threshing. I was twelve years old then. But if Dad had used his head, he could of made a lot of money by manufacturing the first toy automobile ever made, I'm sure." Papa always believed in his inventions!

After Papa's marriage to Mama came the invention of the Magic Pump. Then in St. Louis, Papa invented what he called the Turkish Game Board. Papa persuaded Mama's mother to sign her 160-acre farm in Canada over to him, presumably so he could take out a loan on it to finance his production of the game boards. In return, he gave her stock. But Papa ignored the property tax bills that came from Canada every year, and eventually he lost the farm in Canada because he didn't pay the taxes.

The Turkish Game Board looked like a large tin lid with slots in it. Colored metal strips slid in and out of the slots to create what was really a mechanical tic-tac-toe. Papa got a patent on it and even sold a few. I remember seeing a stack of them on the counter in a five-and-dime store near us, but the game board never went over.

It's too bad that Papa didn't have a financial angel. Then he could have just sat around and thought up things to invent. Somebody should have hired him just for his ideas, because he had tremendous inventive ideas, but no business acumen whatsoever. He was always looking for an easier way to do things. I guess that's how most innovations come about. But after he patented his inventions, he floundered. He didn't have the ability to sell his inventions, and he didn't trust anyone else to do it either.

Papa didn't waste his time and creativity on mundane jobs that just put food on the table. He had grander visions than that. So Papa spent his time not only inventing things, but also talking people into investing in his inventions. He could talk anyone into anything. He was very friendly, always chatting with somebody. He walked around the block and talked to everybody at the stores. We kids got our friendliness from Papa because he loved to converse with people. Mama wasn't bashful, but she wasn't as forward as Papa.

To us Papa was fascinating. Papa always said what he was thinking. When Papa talked, we listened because it was always so interesting. Papa was a lot more fun than Mama. We didn't like Mama then as much as we liked Papa. But we didn't realize as kids that Mama couldn't be anything but grumpy and tired and unpleasant when she scrubbed floors all day for somebody else, then came home and had to cook and wash and bake and iron and take care of the kids and Papa too. When Mama came home, she had her sad face on, and she yelled at us and at Papa because the work wasn't done. Mama wasn't much fun, but Papa was quite entertaining.

> *A Memory from Dorothy*
>
> **I have visions in my mind of Papa lying there, and Mother coming home from scrubbing and saying, "Artur, what are you doing lying there instead of doing something?"**

When we were tiny, Papa put his two fingers on our bellies and walked them up to our necks as if a little bug were crawling on us. As he did that, he said this Serbian ditty:

> *Mala bubitza, trazhe kuchitza,*
> *Evo, evo, evo, evo, evo!*

When he got to the last line, he tickled our necks because the little lost bug had finally found a home! We giggled and giggled. Later Papa did that with all the grandkids, and now they do it with their grandkids.

When Papa noticed something that was a murky gray color, he laughed and said it was *meesh perde farba*. I suppose that's how we learned what the color of mouse poop was! Now, it's a family tradition to call any dark, ugly color *meesh perde farba*.

Papa generally had a happy-go-lucky attitude. He loved to play, and he had a zest for life. When someone did something to annoy him, he often shrugged his shoulders and said, "*Turts miloika!*" and went on with his life. What did he care?

Once Angie and I had white linen dresses that somebody gave to Mama. We thought they were the most beautiful dresses we ever saw. Mama ironed them, and we put them on proudly. Then Papa told us that he would give us a dollar if we didn't get any wrinkles

---

A Memory from Stella

Pop used to tell so many stories that we never knew what to believe. Then Uncle Jim, Mama's brother, said that a lot of the stories about what Papa did as a boy were true. Pop dictated a story to me about his life, and I had to write it out longhand. We would sit in front of the heater when we lived on Hamilton Terrace. He always used to promise me that when he had the book published he'd buy me a fur coat. To this day I do not have a fur coat.

A Memory from Dorothy

Pop always told a different story from what Mother did. When he told a story, Mama would say, "Oh, Artur, it wasn't like that at all." So whether he embellished it or what, I don't know. She would get so disgusted with him.

---

in our linen dresses by the end of the day.

A dollar! That was a huge amount of money. We tried so hard. We walked around with our hands out, we didn't sit down, and we didn't let anybody touch us. We thought we could win the dollar. Mama laughed at us because she knew we couldn't do it. We didn't realize it was impossible not to wrinkle linen. So we never won the dollar, which Papa didn't have anyway because he wasn't working.

Papa told us wonderful stories all the time—stories of his childhood. He liked to describe how he swam in the Blue Danube and how blue the water was. Papa told us that we were gypsies, and we sure looked the part. All of us kids had thick, dark brown hair—loads of it. Whenever he said that about being gypsies, Mama frowned at him as if to say, "Artur, why are you telling them that nonsense?" He taught us the way the gypsies counted to ten: "*Oiney, doiney, treeney, peeney, shava, rava, gonta, gitsel, pitsel, shuck.*" He also told us that we were related to King Peter of Yugoslavia. Claude remembers that Papa even said we were direct descendants of Alexander the Great. Maybe we were royal gypsies!

Papa liked to write too. He wrote a play about the Turks stealing beautiful Serbian girls for their harems. A newspaper woman Papa knew edited it for him, but I wish we had the original in Papa's own words because it was charming. Papa also wrote poems, though none of us was ever sure if they were original or if he copied them from something he read. One that I still have written on a slip of paper in Papa's writing and signed "A.P." is this:

Learning's

We learn of vice and virtue
From very different points:
The good we learn at mother's knee,
The bad at other joints.

Papa wrote down memories from his childhood in Canada, how God had saved him twice from a horrible death—once from a killer horse and the other time from being fed through the spike-pitchers on his steam thresher. Several times Papa experienced what he saw as God intervening in his life. Once it had to do with his health.

In Canada Papa had a mysterious sickness. He got dizzy and shook and had fainting spells, and he couldn't work on the farm for weeks, sometimes longer. Mama later described it as epilepsy, but who knows? Angie always thought that Papa got a head injury breaking those wild horses—that a horse kicked him in the head or maybe he was thrown one too many times. That seemed like a logical explanation to me.

A man from church recommended that Papa go to the Mayo Clinic in Rochester, Minnesota, to find out what was wrong. He even lent Papa the money to go. On the train ride there Papa caught the flu, and he telegrammed Mama to come be with him. She borrowed more money from the same man from church, wrapped her belongings in a sheet and gathered up baby Ruby in her arms. Just before Christmas in 1918, Mama and Ruby boarded the train for Rochester.

After changing trains in Winnipeg, a U.S. customs agent came walking through her car. "Lady, where's your visa?" he asked.

"I don't have nothing, and I don't know anything about it," Mama replied. She didn't know much English, but she understood what he meant. "My husband is sick in Rochester, Minnesota, and he sent a telegram that I should go. He's dying." That's just how she put it. Baby Ruby was lying on the bench beside her. The man looked at her, then went away. Soon he returned with another man.

"Lady, don't you have a visa?" the other man asked.

"No," Mama said. "I don't even know what 'visa' is. I don't know anything about it." So they looked at Mama, and they looked at Ruby, and they let her go on.

Papa recovered from the flu a week after Mama got to Rochester. Then Ruby and Mama were hospitalized with it. They put Ruby in the same room with Mama. That was in 1918 when the influenza became a worldwide epidemic that killed millions of people. People were dying all around them, Mama said, but all the nurses came from every floor to look at Ruby because she was such a beautiful baby!

When Papa recovered from the flu, they started treating him at Mayo Clinic. Mama tells what they finally discovered about Papa in her own unique way: "They couldn't find what was wrong with him. So finally Charlie Mayo himself said, 'There is something wrong with that man, and I'm going to find out what it is.' So they ordered him in one room, and told them to put the heat on all the way to make it just as hot as could be. And him and Papa stayed there. At once, Papa fainted. He said, 'Now I know what is wrong.' He knew right away what was wrong when he fainted.

"They found out that the fluid in Papa's brain was all green. They had to tap that and take all that fluid out and put the fresh fluid in. He couldn't sit down. He had to lay down and put his feet up for three solid months. He couldn't do nothing."

After a month at the clinic, Papa moved into the rooming house where Mama and Ruby were staying in Rochester. He had to lie on his back with his head lower than his feet. Mama was going to stay with Papa until he got well, but a letter arrived from Daka saying that three of the kids as well as he and Katherine were sick with the flu, and there were no neighbors who could come help. Mama reasoned with that common sense of hers, "I can't stay with one sick here, and there's five of them over there sick." So she left Papa and took the train home at the beginning of February 1919.

When Papa was finally ready to leave Mayo Clinic after a two-month stay, he told the Mayo brothers that he didn't have any money. They said, "That's all right, Arthur. We know you'll send it to us when you get it." And they let Papa go home after all that

> ### A Memory from Stella
>
> *I remember hearing that Pop arranged to pay a dollar a month to Mayo Clinic, and that they only charged him forty dollars. Papa and Mama did pay Mayo back. Papa always said, "If I ever make any money from writing these books on my life, I'm going to give something to Mayo Clinic." Well, thank goodness the Mayo Clinic made it on their own!*

treatment, not paying a cent. And, of course, Papa did send the money to them eventually—all of it. He paid back the man from church too.

When Papa finally came home, he couldn't sit up for long. He sat for a little while, then he had to lie down again This went on for weeks, with Papa unable to work. But one day something wonderful happened.

"I will never forget it," Mama recalls. "I think it was the beginning of April, one beautiful morning, sun was shining so beautiful, it was beginning to melt, the snow. He got up, like he always do, thinking he's going to have to go back to bed. But he never went back to bed no more. He got up, that left him. Whatever it was left him right now. And he never was sick anymore, and he never went back to bed no more. He was well from there."

For the rest of his life, Papa never experienced any more symptoms. Mama believed it was a miracle, and I suppose Papa did too.

Papa was a decent man who believed in right and wrong—and he always told us when we were wrong! If one of us did something stupid, Papa said, "*Glupava!*" and hit the offending child on the head. "You dumbbell!" Mama called us that too, at times. Why, sometimes we even hit ourselves on the head and said, "*Glupava!*" when we did something silly! If Papa really got mad at us, he called us *jubra*, which means "dirt." And Papa didn't hesitate to use his strap on us.

But even with Papa's shortcomings, he really did make us believe that fantastic things could happen. For example, Stoeker's was a big department store a few blocks down on Chouteau Avenue, and they had a big limousine in the window—brand new and shiny black. When Papa bought something there, he got to put his name in for a drawing on the car. Well, Papa told us we were going to win that car. So we told all our friends that we were going to win the car because we believed what Papa told us. We absolutely knew that we were going to win it because our father had told us so. When Papa sat around with the men on the block, that's all he talked about. He really believed he was going to win that car.

Papa was at Stoeker's the night of the drawing, and he came home about 9:30 and told us we had won the car! But we never did end up with it. I guess after all his promises, Papa didn't have the nerve to tell us we didn't win. We found out soon enough, though. My friend across the street, Katy, said that her father knew the man who won the car, and it wasn't Papa. We knew then that Papa had fooled us, and we felt very let down.

Yet in a way Papa's faith in the fantastic helped all us kids believe that the impossible was possible.

Papa with the first car he bought, his 1926 Ford touring car, near the Apostolic Christian Church on Angelica Street. He is standing with his foot on the running board, which was a popular stance with people who owned cars.

A Memory from Claude

When I was twelve, Papa let me drive the car while he was with me. I drove down Natural Bridge to church sometimes, and that was several miles. We drove before they had driver's licenses. Those came out in 1935, and they were only twenty-five cents. You went in there, and they literally just felt you, and if you were warm, you got a driver's license. I think they had three lights up there—red, green and amber. If you could tell what the colors were, you got the license.

It gave us some incentive, and we thought, *Hey, maybe I will get rich. I've got to do things to make myself rich.* That's probably why we all became successful.

Papa preceded much of what he told us with, "When we get rich…." We all listened intently when he talked. Sometimes we even sat around on the floor together, and Papa started a sentence, "When we get rich…." Then we kids yelled out the things we wanted when this miracle occurred. I yelled for candy and beautiful dresses and shoes. Well, when you're a child you don't think of the future too much. I just thought of what I wanted right then. But we had a wonderful time just thinking about being rich. If we hadn't been so poor, we wouldn't have thought being rich was so wonderful.

While Mama was out cleaning for others, Papa used to mop the floor and tell us, "When we get rich, I'm going to build us a round house, and it's going to have rooms in it for all of us. It won't need a coal stove. When the sun comes out, its heat will turn the

A Memory from Dorothy

When Papa worked for the streets and sewers department, he had a little Model T Ford, and we called it the Puddlejumper. It was a Model T Ford with a little truck behind it. It belonged to the city, and he couldn't bring it home. He just had it during the day. He was a delivery man—when they needed something, he took it to them. If somebody broke down, he took them a part.

And when he had to go deliver some tools, he came to pick us up and take us for a ride in it. Oh, we thought that was really something. It was the first ride we ever had in a car, I think. That was the biggest thrill!

house around. It will keep turning the house around toward the sun so the sun will keep it warm all the time."

How that picture fired our imaginations! Just think, we wouldn't need coal or wood to burn in the stove because the sun would make our house warm! We drew pictures in our minds of this magic round house that would be warm because the sun would do the work instead of wood or coal. How proud we were of our clever Papa, and we told our friends at school about this magic house! We thought it was utterly unbelievable, but look—today we have solar homes. Sometimes I think that poverty is the true mother of invention.

Everyone on the block lived pretty much as we did, so being poor was just the way life was to us. However, we did have an idea of what being rich would be like.

You were rich...

- ~ if you could buy an ice cream cone that cost three cents.
- ~ if you had a whole apple to eat, not just someone else's leftover apple core.
- ~ if you had a banana on the table at home.
- ~ if you had a dress that wasn't made from the same bolt of material as all your sisters' dresses were.
- ~ if you had shoes that were bought new at a shoe store, not shoes someone gave your Mama because their kids had almost worn them out.
- ~ if you never had to eat lard smeared on bread with salt and pepper on it for dinner.
- ~ if you didn't have to shiver in the winter just because your folks didn't have a quarter to buy a bushel of coal.

We kids decided that a few people on our block were actually rich. The Boriches, for instance, who had the tavern and restaurant across from us—we knew they must be rich because they always had enough food. In fact, they had so much food they even sold it to other people!

—⊶⊷—

*A Memory
from Ruby*

Once Papa went to the shoe store
down the street a few blocks away,
and he bought all of us high-top
shoes for a dime a pair. That was
when people no longer wore high-
top shoes. They were turn-of-the-
century, and this was in the
twenties. They were very much out
of fashion. But we wore them to
school. They were all we had.

—⊶⊷—

And we knew Mr. Bumstead had to be rich because he had so many lovely clothes and shoes and socks and underwear in his store. And people who ran the tiny little confectionery shop near the end of the block—they had to be rich because they had loads of those long white papers with dots of colored candy pasted on them, and oodles of those small tin pans with sugar candy in them. When someone gave us a penny for candy, we used a tiny tin spoon to dig out the candy with. It didn't matter that the rough edges of the tin spoon cut our lips and made them bleed because the candy tasted so good.

And Mr. Art Malone who had the jewelry store at the end of the block—he had to be rich too. We pressed our noses against his window and looked longingly at the beautiful watches and necklaces and rings with all the colored stones in them! Why, Mr. Malone was so rich that he had a tall, black iron clock on the sidewalk in front of his store.

But while we were waiting to get rich, Papa worked here and there and saved where he could. He knew how to do anything. He was very good mechanically because he was a tinkerer. We thought all fathers were that way. So we were very surprised to discover that some fathers didn't even know how to hold a hammer and a nail.

Anytime the soles of our shoes wore out or got a hole in them, we put newspaper or cardboard scraps in the bottom until Papa had a chance to put on new leather soles. He had an iron shoe form, and he slipped the shoe over it. Then he traced the pattern of the sole and drew it onto leather that he bought from the shoe repair shop—nice, smooth light tan leather. Whether our shoes were black or white, they always got a tan leather sole. After he cut out the leather pattern, he hammered the sole onto the shoe with little nails. Papa wasn't an expert, of course, so sometimes the nails came through the soles. Ouch, that hurt! But with the new sole, we could wear the shoes a little while longer,

until they got too tight. Then they were passed on to the next child in the family.

For quite a while Papa went from job to job. After his secondhand store downstairs went broke, he built a little ice cream stand and set it up on Montrose between Chouteau School and our house. He walked to Pevely Dairy to buy the ice cream. (I've still got the ice cream scoop he used, an old-fashioned scoop with nickel gears.) I'm sure he didn't make

Angie and I standing in front of Papa's ice cream and soda stand. Papa built this ice cream stand. He had to have a place of his own.

much money because he had to keep everything iced, and ice was expensive. After that, he opened an ice cream stand in Carondelet Park, where he sold root beer and soda. But he found out he couldn't make any money at it, and soon he quit.

Once Papa was hired at Pevely Dairy. He could walk there, and he was so glad. Out of his first week's salary of twelve dollars he had to buy work boots for nine dollars. Papa and Mama were pretty upset that he had to use so much of his salary on the boots, which he had to leave at the dairy every day. That job only lasted a few weeks—who knows why. Once he came home with a quart of ice cream for part of his salary. Oh, did Mama yell, but we kids were thrilled!

In between doing nothing and having odd jobs, Papa decided he was going to be a

A Memory from Ruby

Papa liked to have his own businesses. When he did get a job and worked for someone else, evidently men liked to tease him. They'd get him mad, and he'd lose his temper. Then he'd lose jobs because of not controlling his temper. I believe he was goaded into losing his temper because we were considered the dark people, the gypsies more or less, because we were all dark-haired with dark eyes.

barber. So he bought all the tools and rented a place and put up a sign: "Haircuts, 25 cents." And people just lined up to get their hair cut for a quarter. But that didn't last long either.

Once Papa got fired from a job for insubordination. Stella remembers that it made the newspaper, and Papa was so eager to see the article. There was his picture with the caption, "Fired for Insubordination." We all wanted to crawl under the table, but Papa was beaming. He thought that was the greatest, to get his picture in the paper.

Strangely enough, the only time Papa had a steady job was during the Depression. He started working for the city of St. Louis sewer department in 1927 and worked there on and off for five years, until the Democrats got in and Republicans like Papa lost their jobs.

During our first few years on Chouteau Avenue, we rarely had enough money to buy food and pay rent too. One day a friend of Papa's came by and announced excitedly, "Arthur, there's a place down here that gives away commodities."

"What do you mean, commodities?" Papa asked. The man told him that meant food. "Well, what do I have to do for it?" was Papa's next question.

"Nothing. They just give it away free."

Papa didn't understand that. It was insulting to him. So he declared proudly, "No, I will never accept anything free. I won't take charity." He would never accept it. He chased the man home.

Papa had his pride. That's the way most folks felt. But while pride caused most people to work harder, it pushed Papa to come up with the one big idea that would make him rich. He believed in himself and his ideas—especially his doll voice.

Chapter Four

'Pa-Pa'

One day Papa was hired to work in the doll hospital at the Famous-Barr Department Store. From that day on, Papa developed an interest in dolls and doll voices that became almost an obsession for him. He worked harder on his dolls than he had ever worked on anything before. It brought out the best in him and the worst in him.

At the doll hospital Mrs. Costello taught Papa to repair broken dolls—the jointed and kidskin dolls that people brought in. That was in the days when people fixed things that broke instead of just throwing them away and getting new ones. Papa became an

Angie and I with our beautiful dolls. Mama always put bows in our hair when she wanted us to look beautiful.

expert at repairing dolls, not stopping until the dolls looked and worked like new again.

Sometimes Papa brought home a doll leg or an arm or a head to repair for a customer who wanted it back the next day. He spread an oilcloth on the kitchen table, and out came all the supplies and tools. Oh, that awful smell of lacquer. We had only two rooms, so we couldn't get away from that smell. But how pleased Papa was when he finished a part! After spending the evening repairing it and painting it just the right color, he held it up for all of us to admire and said proudly, "Doesn't that look real? It looks just like a new one." We all agreed. As we girls fixed our eyes on the dolls Papa worked on, we wished they were ours. It wasn't long before our wishes came true.

When Papa worked on dolls at Famous-Barr, he threw the broken doll parts into a box. One miraculous day the idea hit him to ask if he could have the box of broken parts. When Mrs. Costello said yes, he brought them home and transformed them into dolls for us. He loved to fill in the cracks and repaint the porcelain heads and legs and arms and make new fingers from plaster. He attached repaired legs to hollow torsos, stringing them together perfectly. Mama even helped out, straightening and combing and curling the old matted wigs made of real human hair. She also washed and patched the discarded doll clothes and shoes and stockings. We kids saw Papa and Mama working on the dolls, but we thought the dolls were for Papa's customers.

That Christmas, Papa surprised us with the lovely dolls he had put together. Mine had a porcelain head with beautiful long blonde curls and blue eyes. To us, blonde hair and blue eyes was the acme of beauty because we were dark people. My doll's legs even bent, and she had beautiful clothes. Ah, did I love that doll!

With our lovely dolls in our arms, Angie and I paraded down the street. When our friends saw our beautiful, expensive big dolls, they couldn't believe they were ours! How could our parents buy us dolls that only *rich* people bought for their daughters? Didn't our mother do housework to make enough money just to buy food?

Papa continued to piece together dolls for us. Sometimes one leg was longer than the other because that was all he had, but we didn't know the difference. We loved them just as they were. Papa even put two of the dolls he made in his barbershop. He called them Angeline and Millie, and we felt so proud that he would name his dolls after us!

While Papa worked at Famous-Barr, he became totally enraptured with the voice dolls. However, he felt that a doll should not only say "Ma-ma" when a child turned it over, but the doll should cry for "Pa-pa" too. Weren't fathers as important as mothers? In this way Papa began his long quest to invent and perfect the "Pa-pa" voice box for dolls.

Papa later told Clarissa Start, a reporter for the *St. Louis Post-Dispatch*, that the wishy-washy "Ma-ma" sound was easy for babies to

A Memory from Claude

Papa brought broken dolls home from the doll hospital, and I worked on them—jointed dolls strung together with elastic. Once I stuck a pair of scissors in my finger, and it became infected. That was before the days of antibiotics. The doctor opened up a cut in my finger, and I had to soak my hand in salt water several times a day to try to draw that infection out. It wasn't working, so he had to cut a little deeper down into my hand. He stitched it up rather crudely. Then I had to soak my hand many times a day. Finally the infection went away. But now I have a crooked finger and a scar from that.

say. But the "Pa-pa" word must be forced out, which required a more mature speaking ability. It was equally hard to recreate the "Pa-pa" sound mechanically. With the "Ma-ma" sound, the air could flow through the reeds freely. But the reeds had to close completely to create the puff of air for the "Pa-pa" sound. But Papa was undaunted in his endeavor to create this sound. Every evening he spread his tools and materials out on the oilcloth on the kitchen table and worked for hours trying to create the desired sound. He

Papa proudly showing off a baby doll he put together with his voice box in it.

experimented with brass reeds and bellows, gluing them together, searching for just the right pitch to make the doll cry for her papa.

Often Papa asked us, "What do you think this sounds like?" Then he blew into the reeds and asked, "Does it sound real?"

"No, it doesn't sound like 'Pa-pa' yet," we said. We hated to tell him, but he wanted us to be honest.

Papa built over one hundred voice boxes, struggling for the right sound. He worked on it for several years until he finally got it the way he wanted in 1925.

We all listened excitedly to the final product, then we exclaimed, "Yes, that sounds like the real 'Pa-pa.' That sounds like a little girl really said it!" How proud he was of his invention!

Papa put his treasured voice box into a lovely girl doll with a cloth body, a porcelain head, and porcelain hands and feet. She was beautiful, with blonde weenie curls and blue eyes. But best of all, she not only cried "Ma-ma" when tilted to the left, she also

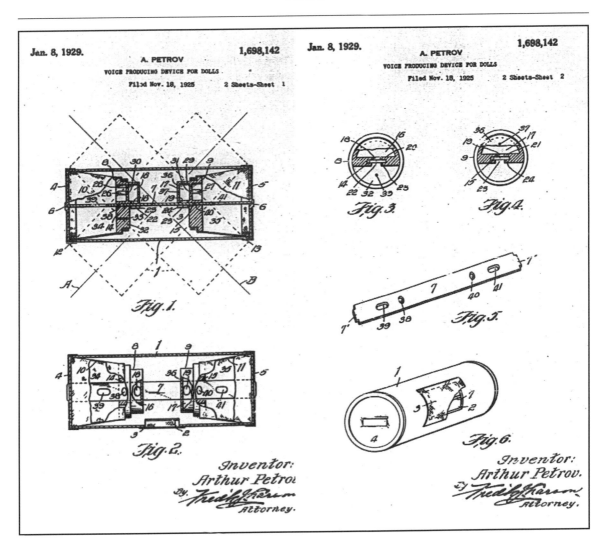

Here is the drawing portion of the patent for Papa's first voice box, which he applied for in November 1925. A year later, in December 1926, he applied for a patent on another type of voice box. Then in August 1927 he applied for a patent on a reed for a voice box. His final application for a patent was in April 1938. That was for the triangular voice box he used in the Bee-Bee Dolls.

cried "Pa-pa" when tilted to the right. Papa realized early on that a doll that tilted to the left and right was much better than one that had to be tipped forward for the voice box to work. When the doll was tipped forward, the child could not see the doll's face. He was clever to notice those details.

Papa carefully placed his finished doll right on top of the *orman* in the kitchen where our underwear and socks and clothes lived. Papa put her up high so no harm would come to her. Then he sternly warned us, "Don't ever touch this doll."

One day after school we were all in the kitchen when seven-year-old Ruby decided to take the doll down. "I just want to hold it," she explained. "I just want to hold it for a minute."

"Don't touch it or you'll get a beating!" Angie warned. But Ruby didn't listen. She pushed the chair close to the *orman,* then she stood up on it. Ruby reached for the cherished doll, but she didn't get a good enough grip on it before she pulled on it. As luck would have it, the doll fell out of her hand and came crashing down, breaking her beautiful porcelain face with the sleeping eyes and blonde curls!

We all gasped, then we moaned. Ruby froze for a second. As soon as she realized what she had done, she burst into tears and ran off to hide under the *dushek!*

Of course, we kids couldn't resist letting her know what was ahead for her. "You're going to get a beating. You're going to get a beating. Wait till Papa comes home. You're going to get a beating," we sing-songed. All of us knew what was coming. We weren't afraid of Papa, but we always got a beating with the strap when we did something wrong. It was just part of life, and afterward we didn't think too much about it. The last time Papa beat me I was seventeen.

Parents treated their children differently then. When I see how some parents love their kids now, it is so much more caring than what we experienced. Mama loved us, but she didn't have the time to spend with us that parents have now, with all our modern conveniences. And children were suppressed then. No one knew or cared what each child's personality was like. Kids didn't find out what they themselves were like until they were older.

Anyway, we couldn't wait for Papa to come home so we could tell him what Ruby had done and show him his broken doll. We were dying to know what he was going to do because we all knew that Ruby was Papa's favorite. We just accepted that as a fact of life—jealousy was unknown in our family. We all knew that Ruby was truly a living *lutka*, an absolute doll with a beautiful dreamlike face and large innocent eyes that melted anyone's heart when she asked for anything—which she seldom did. She didn't complain either. Ruby must have known she was her father's pride and joy, yet she never took advantage of it.

When Papa came home and saw the doll in pieces, he groaned. I remember the expression on his face. He looked sad and mad and disappointed at the same time. He kept saying something in Serbian under his breath.

Ruby was always so honest. As soon as Papa came home she came out of hiding, walked up to him and just stood there with her great big doll eyes wet with tears of remorse. She looked at him with this blank expression on her face, fully thrown onto his mercy.

Dorothy asked Papa when he was going to beat Ruby.

"I'll go get the strap," volunteered Claude, just trying to be helpful.

Papa's heart was broken, but he knew he couldn't beat his precious Ruby. He said, "Not now. Later." We waited all evening for Ruby's beating. We even reminded him before we went to bed, "Aren't you going to give Ruby a beating?"

"Some other time," he grumbled.

Ruby and Dorothy in the park in 1927, a couple years after Ruby broke the doll. Ruby and Dorothy were both very pretty.

"Some other time" dragged on to the next day and the next. Soon it was summer again, and Ruby's beating never came. The years went by and Ruby never got her beating. That's the way it went.

In the meantime Papa repaired the shattered doll. Then one day Papa told us that men from New York were coming to look at his doll and hear his doll voice. We told all our friends on the block about this astonishing event. "I wonder what men from New York look like?" we asked each other. New York may as well have been the moon to us.

The day finally arrived, and Mama dressed us all up in our best clothes. She and Papa dressed up too. The men from New York climbed up the long brown steps to our two rooms. There we all were, standing around the edges in our best clothes, clean faces and hands, gawking at these men from New York. How disappointing it was to discover that they had hands and feet and heads just like Papa! I did notice, however, that their clothes were smooth with no wrinkles in them, and that they spoke as if they had gone to school for a long time.

I whispered to Angie, "That's the way I want to talk. I'm going to talk like that some-day. I'm going to read books, and I'm going to learn to talk that way." Every time I heard anyone speak intelligently, it was a great inspiration to me. I vowed, "I'm going to be that way." Even as a very young girl, I wanted to learn about everything. I wanted to be more than I was. I knew there was more out there than I had at that time, and I knew that speaking well was the key to it all.

Papa was proud of us, so he told the men our names and something about each of us. When he came to Ruby, Papa said, "This one is the prettiest." When it was my turn, Papa told them with a chuckle, "This one is the ugly one." I always hung my head when Papa said that about me, but I knew it was true. I wasn't pretty like my sisters.

Then Papa took down the doll with the voice that said "Ma-ma" and "Pa-pa" and showed it to the men from New York. He also let them look at his voice box that was marked "Pat. Pending." Papa even gave them one to take with them.

The men from New York offered Papa two cents royalty on each voice. Oh, did that upset Papa! I don't think he understood that two cents a voice box inside thousands of dolls was a lot of money. It just sounded like two cents to him. So he declared roughly, "No, I can make millions manufacturing these myself." Papa became very rude, so the men left without making a deal, and that was the end of that. Apparently, Papa decided then and there to manufacture the dolls himself.

Papa worked at Famous-Barr for a couple of years, then he went to work for Scruggs-Vandervoort-Barney, another department store in St. Louis, running their doll hospital. Soon after the men from New York left, he quit Scruggs to start his own doll factory. He named it the St. Louis Doll and Toy Manufacturing Company, and it opened at 704 O'Fallon Street. He had applied for a patent on his cylindrical voice box that said both "Ma-ma" and "Pa-pa" in late 1925, and the application was approved in 1929. There he made the Rock-a-by Doll. After a couple of years, he moved his factory to 15th and Monroe.

We were all so small then, we don't remember much about that first doll factory. Dorothy remembers seeing arms and legs hanging on wires and the smell of lacquer. Claude recalls a visit to the doll factory with Papa. While playing there, Claude sliced his hand open on a razor blade that came up out of a table where ruffles for the dresses were cut.

A Memory from Ruby

One of the lawyers from New York patted me on the head and said to Papa, "Just think, Arthur, you can send this girl to college!" They offered him, I think, a nickel a voice, and he thought that was absolutely stealing from him.

A Memory from Claude

When Papa rejected the businessmen's offer, they gave each of us children a fifty-cent piece, which was a lot of money in those days. "You're going to need it," they told us. "You sure have a stubborn father."

One of Papa's first doll factories. The sign on the corner of the building says, "Makers of Papa Mama Dolls."

Papa quickly wrapped a towel around it and rushed Claude in a streetcar to a doctor. They put seven stitches in, but Claude says it was such a large and deep cut that they would have put twenty-seven stitches in today.

For a while Papa ran the doll factory while he worked for the city during the day. One time he arrived at his office at 420 Market Street to find that the safe had been chiseled open and his doll with the voice had been stolen. The article about the theft in the newspaper said that Papa would "make another model at once to forestall any effort of the thieves to patent the voice box." And it added that "one company told him the device should yield him $100,000 a year in royalties."

I don't know which company that was, if they really said that or if that was Papa's conclusion. Maybe the two cents a voice would have added up to that. Who knows?

Jimmy says that the secretary at that first doll factory ran away with whatever money Papa had, but he's the only one who remembers hearing that. Whether or not that contributed to Papa's doll factory going bust, no one knows. But within a short while, Papa had to shut down his doll factory. He still had his job with the city, but his dream of manufacturing voice dolls would have to wait.

Papa continued to perfect his voice box. Apparently, the first voice box he invented was too large to fit in most dolls, so he worked at designing a smaller one. He created several doll voice boxes of different designs and shapes over the years, and ended up filing several more patents, including one for a triangular box in 1938. Then Papa talked some new people into investing in his doll voice. Those were the days when immigrants came to America and brought wonderful ideas. They started many companies, and people had confidence in them. People thought they would make money by investing in an enthusiastic immigrant's novel idea. Most of the companies in America at that time were started by immigrants. Papa was handsome then too. He smiled all the time when he talked. He could talk people into anything. He even talked a man who won fifty thousand in the Irish sweepstakes into investing in one of his doll factories.

A Memory from Mama

Most of the time Papa didn't work. He was going to make millions all the time, but never got there to make them.

It was almost ten years before Papa realized his dream again. Papa's next doll factory, the Mid-West Doll Manufacturing Corporation, came into being on July 6, 1938, on one of the floors of a large building at 1708 Delmar. It started with capital stock in the amount of twenty thousand dollars, with Papa owning half of it. At least four other investors were involved, purchasing stock for one hundred dollars a share. One bought as few as six shares, and another as many as forty.

Papa's enthusiasm convinced people that he was going to make it this time. We kids were all grown up by then. I was twenty-three and Claude was twenty-one, and we believed in this great venture. So Claude worked on the assembly line that made the voice boxes. Claude's wife, Toni, and I both quit our jobs to work for Papa, and Papa was glad because we had so much sewing experience.

Papa had about six ladies sewing for him, and I was the forelady. We stitched the composition heads and arms and legs to the cloth bodies, then inserted the triangular voice boxes into the torsos. We also sewed the clothes and dressed the dolls. I even designed one of the lined, plush coats. But, oh, how the ladies grumbled about the dress fabric! Papa picked it out, and it was that unmanageable taffeta that frayed easily, and

Here are some publicity photographs of the different styles of Bee-Bee Dolls. Some were girl dolls and some were baby dolls, but they were all called Bee-Bee Dolls.

Here's one of the Fastest-Selling Lines of Dolls, Doll Parts and Doll Accessories Ever Offered!

The bodies of all our dolls are so arranged that they can sit on the edge of a chair or table, and can walk straight forward when held by the hands. All our dolls have human hair - available in 3 colors - Brunette, Tosca, and Blond.

BEE-BEE DOLL #40 A Beautiful 24" Girl Doll. High-grade composition head, arms and legs. Cotton-stuffed body. Beautiful face. Swivel neck. Papa and mama voice. Human Hair (long or short curls.) Sleeping, glace eyes with lashes. Organdie dress, and handsome Velveteen coat in black or red, trimmed with white plush, and with white plush muff.

All Within A Year!

In the short span of a year, the Mid-West Doll Mfg. Corp. has grown from a small, struggling concern, to a large substantial firm doing an international business. This remarkable growth is due to a remarkable doll - the BEE-BEE DOLL - the only doll on the market today that can say both "Mama" & "Papa"! This amazing doll has been a sensation wherever it has been shown - and all smart doll buyers are making sure they will have a big supply on hand for Christmas.

This is the first page of the flyer Papa created for the Bee-Bee Doll.

they could hardly turn a seam on it. It was so difficult to work with, they had to sew the ruffles by hand. We couldn't keep the ladies very long because they were only making six dollars a week, and no one could live on that. I was embarrassed because the workers were so discontented. I sided with them, agreeing that they didn't make enough money.

But Papa wasn't concerned with business details like that. He liked to create, and he kept creating new dolls and new styles. Some of the dolls we made then were baby dolls, and some were what we called girl dolls, like toddlers. But Papa named all them after his youngest daughter, Bee Bee. Since Bee Bee was named after Bee Bee Caram, I think Papa named the dolls as a tribute to her as well.

The Bee-Bee Dolls were not fancy dolls. They almost had a homespun flavor to them. They weren't like Ideal Doll Company dolls or the German dolls that were brought into America with their gorgeous dresses and hairdos and bonnets. Ours were plainer. They were priced from $16.50 to $48.00 per dozen, wholesale.

Papa put up a display of his dolls at Famous-Barr, and I demonstrated them. I had so much faith and confidence in them. The tag on the doll proclaimed, "I walk. I talk. I sleep." Well, they walked if a person guided them along, so that's what I did. When people came up to the display, I explained how the doll said "Ma-ma" and "Pa-pa," and demonstrated how it walked. I showed off the outfits and the different sized dolls we offered.

In the winter of 1938 Papa traveled to New York to promote his doll. He went to the Fifth Avenue Toy Fair and wrote back on a New York skyline postcard: "There is nothing new except the Snow White and the Seven Dwarfs. The dress style is about same as last year. Some dolls are dressed in foreign costumes." After seeing shop after shop in New York, he wrote in his indomitable style, "They got everything in the world to sell here but the Bee-Bee Doll."

Papa manufactured about four thousand Bee-Bee Dolls. He sold them to Blackwell-Wielandy, Famous-Barr, Sears-Roebuck, Stix-Baer & Fuller and several firms outside the St. Louis area. Why, he even received orders from China and India as a result of an advertisement he placed in a toy magazine. But he only produced about 10 percent of the orders he received. He just didn't have enough money to make all the dolls that were ordered. Plus, all the work was being done by hand, so the dolls were produced too slowly.

One of the shareholders offered to bail out the corporation by loaning it eighty thousand dollars, but in return he wanted the majority of the stock. Papa would retain only ten shares. Of course, Papa refused that offer. He wanted to be in control.

Sears-Roebuck negotiated a big Christmas contract with Papa's doll factory in 1939, but Papa was unable to furnish the number of dolls they wanted in time. That made the Sears-Roebuck people upset because they didn't place orders with people who couldn't fill them because it hurt their reputation. So they cancelled the whole order. The Sears-Roebuck representative regretted this, saying in a letter that they would have been able to sell "several thousand dozen."

Through Sears, the Ideal Toy and Novelty Company heard about Papa and wrote to him, asking him if they could sell his doll or perhaps take over the manufacture of the voice under a royalty agreement. Apparently some samples were exchanged, but nothing came of it. Papa quit responding to their requests because he didn't have the materials or money to manufacture any more voices.

That factory lasted a couple of years. After it went under, Papa noticed someone else's ad for a doll that he thought was his, and he initiated a lawsuit. He thought his patent had been stolen. But he never carried it through. Perhaps he came to realize that there were other Mama and Papa voices out there on the market by then.

Papa was naïve, and he mishandled things. It was frustrating for those of us working for him. Once a salesman came in and told Papa that his dolls were so beautiful that he could sell lots of them. So Papa gave him one of every kind. I don't think Papa even took his name. Of course, we never heard from him again. That was the way it always went.

An odd coincidence happened about eight years later.

Right after World War II, Dorothy started going with Ned, a young man she met when they both worked at McDonnell Aircraft. He picked her up at home one night, and Dorothy introduced him. "Mom and Dad, I want you to meet Ned Blades."

Papa responded warily, "Blades? You any relation to Fred Blades?"

"Well, yes, he's my father."

With that, Papa and Mama looked at each other as if saying, "Oh, my gosh!" Dorothy wondered what it all meant. But she and Ned went out on their date.

The next day Papa told her, in an important manner, "Dorty" (that's how Papa pronounced her name), "I want to tell you something about Fred Blades." Then he told her that Fred Blades had been one of several prominent attorneys who had invested in the doll factory. They set up a company to make the voice, but when the company failed, the investors lost all their money.

A Memory from Dorothy

Papa could not compete. He didn't know how to do it. He had no business sense, and he was ignorant of big company ways. His idea was, "If I can invent it, I can run it." But every company he had, failed. Papa was impulsive, and as his lawyer said, "You always come to me after you've signed something. Then it's too late. You should come to me before you sign it." Papa would sign anything. He believed everybody. He was so gullible. He believed people were going to do just what they said.

Mama didn't save the dolls from the doll factory. Every doll factory Papa had cost friends and relatives money. She hated it. It was all bad because every one of them failed, and she tried to work and pay back money that he borrowed from their relatives. He was always borrowing, and he wouldn't tell her, and then she found out. She hated it so much, I'll bet she thought, "I'm going to get rid of all these dolls."

"Everybody was pretty nice about it," Papa continued, "but Fred Blades grabbed me by the neck and put me against the wall. He was going to beat the pulp out of me because I lost his money."

Then Dorothy married Ned! Sometime after the wedding Fred told Dorothy his version of what had occurred. "Dorothy, I'd like to clear up some things with you about your dad and the doll." Apparently, when the investors realized that Papa was going to fail and the company was going down the drain, they made a deal with a voice company for a certain royalty amount for each voice box. They planned on contracting with another doll company to manufacture the dolls. The investors didn't tell Papa what they were doing because they knew he wouldn't go for it. They wanted to get it all set up and then tell him.

But Papa got wind of it and went to the other company and queered the whole deal. He

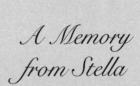

A Memory from Stella

After most of us were grown, Pop convinced a group of people in New Baden, Illinois to invest in a doll factory. Pop wanted to sell the house and use the money for the factory. Mother said no, she wouldn't sign. She had her name on the house—finally. Thank goodness, because that factory went under too. Pop was a salesman, but not a businessman.

thought they were stealing his patent. Papa wanted to be in charge of everything, even when he had no expertise in that area. Claude says that Papa would always say, "This is my baby and I'm going to nurse it." That's the expression he used, and that thinking lost him opportunities.

"Fred Blades said that we all would have been millionaires if Papa hadn't done that," Dorothy remembers. "And I have a feeling that we would have, but it wasn't meant to be, I guess. A few years after Ned and I were married, one Christmas Fred gave Papa the voice box that he still had in his safety deposit box. That was kind of sweet, I thought."

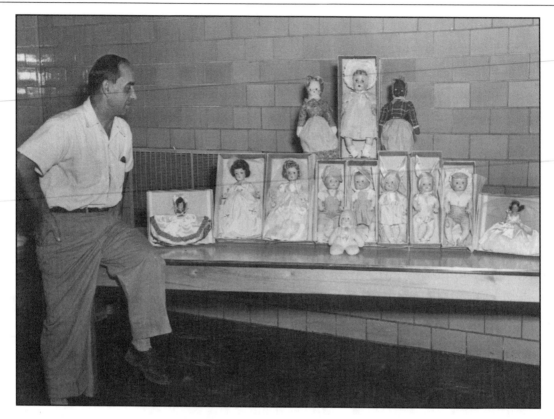

This 1948 photograph shows Papa with his new line of dolls
at the Plastic Doll and Toy company in Illinois.

Even after Mid-West Doll Manufacturing Corporation failed, Papa's dream of a successful doll manufacturing company would not die. In 1946 he started a new doll factory across the river in New Baden, Illinois. At first, they put together little rag dolls, but later they manufactured real dolls, using sawdust and glue to make the bodies. Local people sewed the clothes. Then the voices were added. Papa also made a topsy-turvy doll that he called Julie Ann, the Dual Doll.

Several men invested in the Plastic Doll and Toy, Incorporated. At some point they ordered clothes and eyes and other parts from different manufacturers, but they didn't have enough money to pay the C.O.D. bills. That company went belly up too, and again the investors lost their money.

Even with all his missed opportunities, Papa did bring something into the doll world by inventing that voice. But sadly, he never succeeded at manufacturing it and getting it out to the little girls of the world.

However, Papa was too egotistical to think that he was a failure. He always thought something else or someone else caused his endeavors to fail. He would have made it, *but....* He could have been successful, *except for....* I don't think he ever realized he had no business insight at all. He did everything from the heart, not from the mind. His enthusiasm made him optimistic that his next venture would succeed. That optimism always attracted investors, and the investors always lost their shirts.

Meanwhile, Mama scrubbed other people's floors and washed other people's clothes to feed us and pay our rent.

Chapter Five

Scrubbing Floors

The rent at 2943 Chouteau Avenue in 1921 was nine dollars a month. When the landlord came to collect the rent money, Mama gave him what she had. Sometimes it was only fifty cents.

The night before the landlord came, Papa and Mama talked about how they didn't have the rent money—again. Papa wasn't home the next day to explain it to the landlord. Where he was I don't know, but Mama was always the one who had to apologize, explaining that her husband hadn't found work yet and, of course, she had to hold a few cents back for food for the children.

I was standing next to Mama one time when she answered the landlord's knock. I looked up to see a tall man who had on a winter coat and a hat. All the men wore hats in those days, regardless of where they went. They wore real hats, not the baseball caps men wear today.

Mama was embarrassed to have to tell him they didn't have the rent, but the landlord was very nice about it. He must have been a compassionate man because I watched him respond quietly and softly. I suppose many tenants in those days couldn't pay the entire rent at one time. Mama told him that hopefully she would have another fifty cents or a dollar in a week, and he always accepted that. I suppose he knew that we were honest people. Most people were honest—especially the people on our block. All the immigrants, like us, were trying to get ahead. We worked hard for our money, and we would never think of cheating anyone out of anything.

When Papa came home, Mama told him that the landlord said they needed to come up with the money as soon as possible. What else could the landlord say? And somehow, by the end of the month, Papa and Mama did manage to pay him the enormous sum of nine dollars, even though it took the landlord quite a few trips to collect it.

Mama's mother was visiting us from Canada once when we were behind three months' rent. She told the landlord she would pay all the back rent. Boy, was he surprised. "I thought I'd get something," he said, "but I never thought I'd get it all at once."

While Papa was inventing things and opening and closing companies and occasionally working, Mama was scrubbing floors for people to make a living. When my daughter and I went to the Ellis Island Immigration Museum in 1994, we saw a life-sized photograph of an immigrant woman scrubbing floors. I was so touched by it that I had to hold on to a post so I wouldn't faint. I couldn't stop crying, thinking of how hard Mama worked and sacrificed for us. She made just two dollars a day, and some days she couldn't get any work, so she didn't make any money.

Mama toiled all her life, even as a child. Back in Eastern Europe, she and her parents and three brothers lived in a square mud house with a dirt floor on an acre of land, on which they grew their food. Quite a few years ago my Uncle Tom called me from

Canada. He had grown up in Hungary and knew the area well where Mama's family was from. "Be sure to see *Fiddler on the Roof*," he said, referring to the new movie that had just come out. "That's just the way your Mama and her family lived." When I saw it, I finally realized what life was like for her then.

Mama and her mother, Militza, wove their own cloth. I have a peasant blouse Mama made from material she wove. A horse thrashed the wheat out back by walking over it. Mama's mother washed clothes in a nearby creek. There was a toilet area outside near the house, with a pile of corncobs to use as toilet paper. If they ran out of fresh corncobs, Mama said they just used the old ones over again!

Mama's given name was Smilia, but she was called Moda. She went to school full time for six years. Then she went twice a week for the next two years, finally graduating from the eighth grade. The rest of the time Mama worked in the field from dawn to dusk. Being the oldest daughter, she also helped with the cooking and cleaning and taking care of the children.

At Christmas Mama's parents used to lay straw on the dirt floor and hide nuts in it for the children to find. Sometimes when Mama or one of her brothers misbehaved, her mother made them kneel on dried corncobs as punishment until they cried so much that they were finally allowed to get up. Mama's mother never went to school at all, and she couldn't read or write. As an adult she signed an "X" for her name and had someone wit-

A Memory from Dorothy

Mama said that in the old country the animals stayed in the house like they did. They had a straw floor and a hardened straw roof. They were poor peasants, and nobody owned much land. That's why they were so thrilled when the Canadian Pacific Railroad came over and told them they could own sections of land in Canada. To them that was heaven—to think that they could own land!

A Memory
from Angie

Mama told me that when she was young back in Yugoslavia, she loved to watch the gypsies play their music and sing and dance. She would sneak out at night to go to the woods to watch them. She was creeping back late one night when her Mama caught her and warned her, "Never go there. The gypsies steal children."

ness it. When she received a letter from the old country, she had to have another Serbian read it to her. Militza had three other children who died, but no one knew how old they were or whether they came before or after Mama.

Next door lived Mama's grandparents. One day her grandfather came home with a stab wound he got during a brawl in a tavern, where the men of the village gathered to drink *rakiya* and *shljivovitza*, and he died.

Mama's father, Mladen Trifunov, wanted better opportunities for his family, so he made plans to move to the New World. He and a couple of other men left their little village and booked passage on a ship headed for North America, going ahead to make a way for their families. But after Mladen left, his family didn't hear from him. A year passed, then two. One day a neighbor woman came running over shouting, "Militza! Militza! Your husband is back! He's at the tavern, bragging about where he's been!"

Well, Militza marched down to the tavern to find her long-lost husband and make him come home. When all the explaining had been done, it turned out that he had boarded the wrong ship. Perhaps he didn't know where to go because he could only read Cyrillic and the signs were written in our alphabet. However it happened, he ended up in Argentina instead of Canada, and he had to work there for two years just to make enough money to purchase a ticket back home! What those people went through back then just to give their families a better life!

Mama's parents started saving again, and a year later they sold everything and left their village of Jarkovac for Canada—this time together. Mama was almost seventeen when they arrived in Regina, Saskatchewan, in May 1910. "We didn't know nobody," Mama remembers. "We arrived in Regina, and my father said, 'You all stay at the train station here. I'm going to look for Serbians.'" He returned hours later with a Serbian man, and they stayed with him for their first few days there.

Everyone in Mama's family had to find work in Regina. Her father worked in town and also on a farm. Her mother cleaned houses. Two of Mama's brothers, Jim and Mac, went to work for the local newspaper, the *Regina Leader-Post*. Mama worked in the Regina Steam Laundry, ironing clothes on a mangle. She earned seven dollars a week for

My mama, Moda Trifunov, at the age of seventeen.

five and a half days of work, giving it all to her mother for the family's expenses. If she worked overtime, she got to keep that extra money for herself. Mama made girlfriends at work and enjoyed herself at Serbian dances. Though she was working, it wasn't like the backbreaking labor of the old country. But as soon as she married Papa, the toil began again—farming and having babies and, on Chouteau Avenue, cleaning houses to support her children.

When I picture Mama now, I see her cooking in the kitchen. She was always busy working—either at other people's houses or at our own—yet I never heard her complain. But we kids never played with Mama or went anywhere with her—at least, *never* is how I remember it. When I try hard, I can bring to mind a few times that we went on picnics with her. But she just didn't have the luxury of spending time with us.

When we lived on Chouteau Avenue, Mama worked for Mrs. Palazzolo, who lived on our street. Angie and I walked down to collect her basket of dirty clothes, then we brought it back. After Mama washed and ironed the clothes, we returned them. One day when Mama was sorting those dirty clothes she found a gun in the basket. "Put everything back," she announced abruptly. "Take it back to Mrs. Palazzolo, and tell her I'm never washing her clothes again."

We knew something bad was happening, so we obeyed Mama and immediately took the basket of unwashed clothes back to Mrs. Palazzolo. After we told her what Mama said, oh, was Mrs. Palazzolo upset! She ran down the street to our house. "Moda, I don't know how that happened," she swore. "I don't know where that gun came from." She didn't want Mama to stop washing clothes for her. Mama wasn't so sure that Mrs. Palazzolo didn't know anything about the gun, but Mama finally agreed to continue washing her clothes.

Once Mama earned twenty dollars for crocheting two pair of curtains for Mrs. Borich, Katy's mother across the street. Then a woman from church—the one we stayed with when we had first arrived in St. Louis—told Mama that Papa had borrowed twenty dollars from her. She was going to bring it up at church if he didn't pay her back. So Mama gave the woman her hard-earned twenty dollars to pay Papa's debt.

Mama also cleaned and ironed for Mrs. Rameseri, a woman who lived above her saloon and garden restaurant on the corner of Park Avenue and 18th. Stella recalls that Papa borrowed three hundred dollars from her and couldn't pay it back, so Mama worked it off! Sometimes Mama took little Stella with her when she cleaned there. Stella still remembers Mrs. Rameseri's beautiful marble bathroom and the smell of Lifebuoy soap.

Mrs. Rameseri had beautiful black hair and wore lovely makeup and jewelry all the time. She had a deep husky voice, the same as we Petrovs do. People would come to the bar and say, "Mary, I'd like to buy you a drink." She poured herself a little bit—for all I know she poured water into her glass—and she stood there and sipped it as she talked. She was very friendly with everybody. Men gathered around her, listening to her interesting conversation. She was a fine and decent woman.

Angie, Millie, Claude, Ruby, Dorothy, Jimmy
and baby Stella at the park in 1923.

Because she was Serbian like Mama, Mrs. Rameseri was a friend of Mama's as well as her employer. She was always so sweet to us. Occasionally our whole family was invited to dinner at her house. That's when we got the thrill of seeing her upstairs home. I thought it was the most beautiful place ever. It was very elegant, full of figurines and Italian statues and beautiful dishes, the likes of which none of us had ever seen before. Her draperies were silk, and all the furniture was carved. Maybe seeing that fairyland gave me my taste for the ornate. Later in life I couldn't get enough of Italian ceramics and elegant old-fashioned paintings and and hanging tapestries.

If Mama wasn't out cleaning somewhere, she was at home ironing clothes for Mrs. Barretta. Angie and I and sometimes Claude had the responsibility of taking the clean and pressed clothes back to Mrs. Barretta. We had to get on the streetcar, the Belt Line No. 28, with the crisp clothes that Mama had wrapped loosely in newspaper. When we delivered the clothes, Mrs. Barretta always gave us a couple of pennies or a piece of candy from her confectionery.

One summer day Mama wanted Angie and me to take two bundles of washed and ironed clothes back to Mrs. Barretta. Each of us grabbed a big bundle, and we climbed onto the streetcar. But when we arrived at our stop and stepped off, the clothes slid out

*A Memory
from Stella*

When Mom cleaned for the woman who had the confectionery, Mom also did her laundry. She had to wash the clothes in the basement, then climb all the way up to the third floor to hang the clothes. Mom said she was always so glad when it came time to scrub the floor because she could be down on her knees. She didn't have to be standing.

of the newspaper onto the dirty street. Frantically, we wrapped them back in the paper with the help of a sympathetic stranger. Then we made our way to Mrs. Barretta's house and rang her doorbell, sobbing. When she answered, we explained what happened with tears streaming down our faces. Oh, thinking that Mama would have to wash and iron those clothes again just broke our hearts! Plus, we knew we'd get into trouble. So we begged Mrs. Barretta, "Please don't tell our Mama and Papa!"

"I won't," she promised. "Now don't you worry about it." She paid us the money anyway, whatever Mama charged (it was always change, so it must not have been much). Then we hurried home. We gave Mama the money and never told her what happened. Wasn't that nice of Mrs. Barretta not to get mad?

On Saturdays Mama cleaned house for Mrs. Barretta. At the end of the day, how eagerly we watched for Mama from the front room window. When we caught a glimpse of her tired body stepping off the streetcar, we all raced to the door to meet her because we knew that Mrs. Barretta always sent Mama home with a little bag of stale candies.

When Mama spilled out the small brown bag on the table, red candy squares with flowers inside and jelly beans and hard marshmallow peanuts and broken suckers and marshmallow cookies covered with chocolate were ours for the grabbing. Such tastes as these we had never known before! What did stale mean to us?

Many late afternoons we waited for Mama to come home from cleaning someone's house. When we thought it was about time for her streetcar, we carried our baby sister Stella down to the street. We walked back and forth, down the block and up the block, up the block and down the block, taking turns carrying Stella. I guess we didn't know how to tell time because it seemed like we paced out there for hours waiting for Mama. Often Stella wouldn't stop crying. I kept saying to myself, "Now, when I get to the front of our house the streetcar will stop and Mama will get out. Then I can give Stella to Mama." It seemed to take so long for Mama to come home.

Sometimes we watched for Mama from the front room window. St. Louis winters seemed much colder then, and often the windows frosted over. I pressed my ten warm fingertips against the windowpane until the frost melted. Then I could look down though the clear holes they made to see if Mama had stepped off the streetcar yet.

When a streetcar came and went and Mama didn't get off, I cried because I was sure she wasn't coming back. Then I didn't even want to eat. Nothing interested me when I had that feeling that Mama wasn't ever coming home. I wedged myself between the icebox and the *orman* and cried and cried.

When Mama finally did come home, oh, was I glad to see her! She yelled at me when she saw that I had been crying again. "What are you crying for? I always come home." She slapped me hard, but I was so glad she was home that I didn't care if she whipped me. When Mama was there, everything was all right. And if Mama was happy, it seemed that the sun shone even at night. But most of the time she wasn't happy. She was usually tired and hungry, and she had to settle the crying baby, then make supper for all of us and wash clothes and—oh, my God. What a job she had!

By the time Mama was twenty-eight, all of her teeth had been pulled. No one remembers why that happened to her so young. I guess it was cheaper then to have teeth pulled rather than to have them fixed. She wore dentures for the rest of her life, which must have added to her discomfort.

Because Mama worked so hard, we kids, in our own way, tried to do nice things for her. The linoleum on the kitchen floor was worn out, and the boards underneath showed through. One day I said to my brother and sisters, "Let's not walk on any of the

A Memory from Claude

Angie was a very caring person. She wanted to help everyone and anyone as much as she could. She went out of her way to do things for us kids, and we didn't treat her right. As we got older, we asked her to forgive us several times.

A Memory from Ruby

Angie was so good to all of us. She took such good care of us. I can't tell you how wonderful she was to us.

worn-out places. Let's walk all along the edges so we won't wear out the linoleum any more." We wanted to surprise Mama by saving wear and tear on the linoleum, so we all tiptoed around the worn pathways. But Mama was too tired to notice what we were doing, and we soon bored of our little game and quit.

Angie, being the oldest, was put in charge of all of us when Papa and Mama were gone, especially during the day when Mama was working. I don't know where Papa was. Being in charge of all of us was quite a burden for Angie. She never got to be a child herself. But we didn't understand that as children. We just thought Angie was mean because she made us toe the line. We used to gather in the corner and talk about how unkind she was to us. And she wasn't unkind, of course, now that we look back on it. But we played tricks on her. We didn't like her because she bossed us around, so we were often ugly to her.

Once Thelma Watson and I were doing something we shouldn't have, and Angie got a broom and chased after us. We ran downstairs, and she followed us all the way down the block, shaking that broom at us. When Mama came home, we tattled on Angie. Mama often yelled at Angie because she was the one in charge. Our snitching on her just added to Angie's problems, and she cried. But sometimes Mama took Angie aside and spoke with her gently because she knew that watching us was such a big job.

We kids took a bath once a week on Saturdays, whether we needed one or not! Angie supervised the bathing while Mama was at work. In the summertime Angie brought in a big tub from the back porch and set it down in the middle of the kitchen floor. She heated the water on the stove, then scooped it out with a pan and poured it into the metal tub. The youngest child went in first. Angie scrubbed her, then pulled her out and dried her off. The next one bathed in the same water. By the time it was Angie's turn, six or seven of us dirty kids had already bathed in that water. Angie had to scoop the scum off the top of the water before she could get in. She said that it wasn't fair to be last all the time!

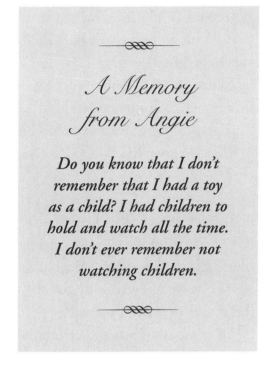

A Memory from Angie

Do you know that I don't remember that I had a toy as a child? I had children to hold and watch all the time. I don't ever remember not watching children.

Angie liked a boy from down the street. He was her age—about ten or eleven. Once when Angie was giving us all baths he came over to talk to her. He just sat around and watched us all get baths. I didn't like it at all that he was there. When we told Mama, she yelled at Angie for letting him in while we were taking baths.

In the winter when we got out of the big metal tub, we put on clean long underwear. The metal buttons were so cold! Once I inched real close to the stove so I could warm my buttons. I held out one button right next to the stove. But it got red hot, and I had to let go of it quickly. When I did, it burned my belly. Oh, that hurt so bad! I tried to shimmy out of those long underwear so fast, but it wasn't fast enough. For years and years I had a square scar from that red hot button. I may still have it.

When I stop to think of how many older children took care of the younger ones in those days, it's amazing more disasters didn't occur. Sometimes I look back with wonder at how fortunate we were. From my point of view, we were obedient kids. We never played out in the street where streetcars and carts and horses went by, and we always stayed away from the Missouri Pacific trains in the back yard. But I know God watched over us because He knew Papa and Mama couldn't be there all the time.

When Mama wasn't working for someone else, she had an endless amount of cleaning to do at home. Besides the housework there was the big job of washing clothes. Papa and Mama didn't buy ready-made soap as it was five cents a bar. So they even had to make the soap Mama used for washing!

Making soap was a big project. First Mama melted all the old lard that was left over from frying. Then she strained it to get all the pieces of food out. Next, some magic ingredient was added—I suppose it was lye. Oh, the odor of that soap mixture on the stove was awful! We all went outside because we didn't like the smell. When we decided it was safe to go back into the house, there was the soap sitting on the sink in blocks.

When Mama was ready to wash clothes, Papa brought in the big copper boiler and the round tubs from the back porch. (Once somebody on Chouteau Avenue gave us a lot of corn, and Papa and Mama boiled the corn in that big boiler until it looked like hominy. We ate that corn for a long time.) Mama set the copper boiler on our coal-burning stove and filled it with water, a pan full at a time. Then she heated the water.

Papa scraped shavings from the homemade soap into the boiler. As the water heated, the soap melted to make sudsy water. First Mama scrubbed all the stains out of the clothes on the washboard. Then she put the white clothes into the boiler. Mama never washed white clothes without boiling them. She and Papa used a stick to stir them around and get them out. If we were helping her, we often burned ourselves with the hot water. But Mama didn't because she was used to hot water.

The other two tubs had cold rinse water in them, one with bluing added. I never understood what bluing did, but Mama said it made the clothes smell better and look better. So Papa and Mama rinsed all the clothes in the clear water first, then the bluing. Then they both wrung out the clothes and hung them out to dry in the back yard—or on the porch in the winter. Later on we had a hand wringer. What a boon that must have been for them!

Mama and Papa talked all evening as they were washing clothes together, mostly about the *stari krai*, the old country where they had both grown up. Then Papa told her what he did that day and where he went. Sometimes they even laughed together.

Another one of Mama's constant responsibilities was making and baking bread. We had bread for breakfast, bread for lunch and bread for dinner. A few times a week before she went to bed Mama made dough. She formed it into loaves and set them out to rise all night. Then, early in the morning, she baked the loaves in the big cast iron stove before she went off to work.

Mama's big cook stove was blue enamel with chrome trim. It had four burners with iron lids that Mama lifted off with a handle in order to drop pieces of wood into the fire. She

A Memory from Dorothy

I helped Mother hang the clothes up in the back yard. I took the clothes out of the basket and handed them to her, and she hung them up. I was there just to hand them to her because it hurt her back to lean over. I wasn't big enough to hang them up myself.

used wood if we didn't have money for coal. All the children on the block went through the alleys looking for scraps of wood. Sometimes we found a wooden box that a store threw out, and we took it home for firewood. But we didn't always get to things first. Other kids needed scraps too.

Attached to the side of the stove was a deep pan that Mama kept full of water so we would always have warm water on hand. We all had to shush our hands in the water before we went to bed. The stove had a couple of gas jets too, but Mama didn't use them much because gas cost money. Oh, the smell of that gas gave me such a headache!

Mama baked the bread in our coal stove in pans that made very large slices. We knew we were home when the aroma of Mama's delicious bread met us at the bottom of the stairs! For our supper we often spread a slice of bread with white lard, then sprinkled it with salt and pepper so that it looked like a design on a large picture.

Mama loved the white bread she made in America. She and Papa talked about how soft it was. She even wrote her cousins in Yugoslavia about how wonderful it was that she no longer had to make bread out of "black wheat" (that's what she called the coarse flour they ground at the local mill from the grains they grew back in Yugoslavia). Here in America she could buy soft white flour, and it made the most delicious soft white bread. Mama loved that white bread till the day she died. Of course, we all know now that black bread is better for us. The people in the old country didn't realize how lucky they were. But, like Mama, I still love soft white homemade bread.

Claude remembers that, with all the things she had to do, Mama sometimes forgot about the bread in the oven, and it burned. But she would tell us, "Eat the burnt parts anyway. They will give you rosy cheeks." So we all fought for the blackened ends!

We didn't waste anything. When Mama made bread she fried the little scraps of leftover dough in delicious hot lard, and we put sugar on them. My, they were such a treat! We ate them till we were full. When Claude ate two pieces, he said he was full up to his knees. Ruby ate a few more pieces and said she was full up to her *guzitza*. To us kids our bodies were empty shells, and when we ate we filled up, starting at our feet and filling up to our necks.

Sometimes Mama sent Angie and me to the bakery at the end of the block to buy seven cents' worth of yeast for making bread. Mama didn't use dry yeast. I don't even know if they had dry yeast then. Yeast was sold in a block. The baker cut off the right amount, usually a chunk about two inches square, and wrapped it in white crinkly paper. As soon as Angie and I walked out the door with the yeast, we opened it and ate little pieces from the ends. Oh, how we loved the taste of yeast! By the time we got home there was very little yeast left.

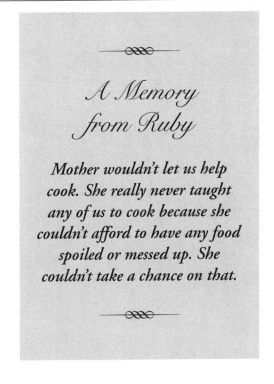

A Memory from Ruby

Mother wouldn't let us help cook. She really never taught any of us to cook because she couldn't afford to have any food spoiled or messed up. She couldn't take a chance on that.

Once Mama went to the baker's to ask why he gave us such a small block of yeast for our money. That's when she found out what really happened. When she came home, she yelled at us for eating the yeast.

We always sat down to supper together, and Mama spread a tablecloth on the table. Most of the time it was oilcloth, but on Sundays she spread out a real cloth one. We always had bread around the house, and we always had jelly, so sometimes we had bread and jelly for dinner. Once Mama bought a dime's worth of bologna and fried it. My brother Jimmy loved that. As an adult he still loved a sandwich of fried bologna and jelly.

Mama made a lot of ingenious dishes using what we could afford, and many of those simple meals have become my favorites. We always thought Mama's cooking was Serbian, but later we realized it had Hungarian influence too. Some nights Mama made cooked cabbage with paprika and onions. It was made like *paprikash*, but with no meat.

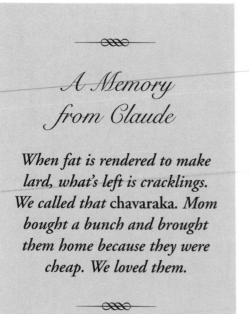

We also loved sliced tomatoes and onions with salt. That was our whole dinner—just a bowl full of raw tomatoes and onions—but was it delicious! Sometimes we had *mandara* for dinner—bread with gravy that Mama made out of the leftover grease the Carams gave us from their restaurant.

Meat was a rare treat for us. How we fought over what we called *kazhuda*, the cooked skin of a pig. We loved to chew on it. I never remember having ham, but we sure enjoyed the pig's skin and bones!

In the winter Mama bought raw bacon and put it outside on the back porch high up where the stray cats couldn't get it. When it froze, Papa brought it in and used the sharp knife to cut it up into little pieces. We all ate it raw with bread. I guess that's where I got my taste for *slanina*, as we called it. Oh, I thought that was delicious. To this day when I buy raw bacon I cut off a piece and chew it up before I cook the rest. I love the taste.

On special occasions Mama picked out a chicken at the store, putting her hands into the chicken cage and feeling which one was fat. The store clerk tied the chicken's legs together, and Claude carried it home with its head hanging down. Papa chopped the head off, and Mama put the chicken in a big pan of hot water to loosen the feathers. Boy, did that smell awful! Whichever child was home had to pull the feathers off. That was the dirtiest job of all because the smell was so terrible. The feathers in the wings were the longest, and they were the hardest to get out. Finally the chicken was ready for Mama to cut up and fry.

When we had company for dinner once, Mama fried a chicken. True to the Serbian tradition, the adults ate first, and we kids stood around at a distance and waited.

Whatever was left we got to eat. Watching the adults eat, we moaned to ourselves, "Oh, I hope they don't eat that piece. Oh, I hope they leave that piece." When they were finished, Papa gave us the signal that we could come to the table. We rushed to the leftovers and hungrily finished them off.

Nothing was better than running home after a day of hard playing at Buder Playground and bounding up the long brown stairs to the aroma of *rezanitza za lukas*—a simple meal Mama made from onions and noodles seasoned with paprika. Sometimes it wasn't ready yet, and that wonderful smell made it hard for us to wait. Perhaps it was so delicious because Mama made her own noodles with eggs and flour and a little salt. First she used an *oklagiya* Papa made from a broom stick to roll out the noodle dough real thin. Then, starting at one edge, she

A Memory from Angie

Once when Mama was sick, she told me to make chicken soup for a sick neighbor. She told me how to make the soup from her bed. I picked up the whole chicken and washed it and put it in the pot. I didn't think of cutting it up. As poor as she was, she was doing that for somebody else. She was so sweet.

rolled the dough up like a newspaper. Next she cut thin slices off the roll with a knife that Papa kept really sharp. (That was the man's job—sharpening all the knives.) Mama unwound those slices to make long noodles, which she hung on the backs of chairs to dry.

Mama also used the kitchen table to cut out patterns and do her sewing. Once Claude was eating noodle soup, and he felt something sharp in the last spoonful of noodles. It turned out to be a couple of straight pins that were left on the table and somehow got stuck in the noodle dough! Oh, was Mama upset that she was so careless!

Sometimes Mama put the soft noodle dough in her hands and rolled off little pieces into hot milk to cook. It became noodles and gravy. We called it *tarana*, and we liked it a

A Memory from Ruby

When we were really poor and we didn't have much food in the house, we had rezanitza za lukas. *When we had those noodles with onions, we knew that things were bad. Papa and Mama wouldn't take help. People from the city came to the house to offer government help, but I remember my mother saying, "No, no, no! We don't need any help!"*

A Memory from Angie

When Mama made noodles, it was a big event. She rolled out the noodles and cut them. Then she put clean sheets on the beds and laid the noodles on the beds to dry. She made a lot of noodles so she wouldn't have to make them often, and they were drying everywhere.

lot. I never knew that anyone else made *tarana* until last year when my niece Karin sent me a package of tiny little bits of dough like Mama's. It was from Hungary, and on the outside of the box was the word "*Tarana*."

On Saturdays Mama made what came to be known as Saturday soup. It was a brothy soup, made with string beans, a little piece of pork and some tomatoes and paprika, and was it delicious! Today we call it string bean soup. Most of us learned to make it—even Jimmy.

When Mama bought a soup bone, she looked for one with lots of *mozhak*. How we fought over that marrow! We ate it out with a spoon, then used a knife to get the little bits that were left stuck to the bone. When Papa finished with a bone—any bone—there wasn't enough left for a dog. He sucked the little bits of meat off it, then he sucked the marrow out of it. He kept that habit all his life.

On Chouteau Avenue Mama made her delicious Serbian chicken soup, and all she could afford were chicken necks and feet. We put the feet into boiling water to loosen the yellow skin, then peeled the skin off and threw away the claws before Mama put the feet into the soup. We all sat around the table waiting for the soup to be ready. Then Mama put the soup in a big pan and set it in the middle of the table. She ladled it out, and we each got a bowl full. Today I make Mama's chicken soup, but it just doesn't taste as good as hers. I water it down too much because I want so much soup!

Deka and Papa would *serche* the soup. They made so much noise eating it, especially sucking all the *mozhak* out of the chicken neck. There was nothing left but some pitiful little bones when they were through. We thought that if you didn't *serche* the soup, you didn't like it. But later we realized that in polite society, people didn't make noise when they ate. That wasn't as much fun.

As young children it didn't occur to us how wonderful Mama really was, how self-sacrificing and hard-working. Everything she did to make our lives pleasant we took for granted. Mama scrubbed and cleaned and cooked from sunup until the time she fell into bed. And on top of that, it seemed as if Mama was always pregnant. Of course, people never talked about it then. Nobody ever told us, "You're going to have a brother or a sister." All of a sudden you just saw a baby. We children thought it was strange to see a woman who didn't have a baby in her arms. Mama was always juggling a baby. Poor Mama, we never saw her rest unless she was sitting in the rocking chair, nursing a child.

In 1929 when I was fourteen, Mama was pregnant again—for the last time. That's when Mama told Papa, "I'm not working anymore."

And she didn't.

Chapter Six

All About Mama

One day as I was playing outside I wondered for the first time how old Mama was. I ran up the dark brown stairs and found Mama in the kitchen with the other kids all around her. "Mama, how old are you?" I asked.

She was surprised at my question, but she answered simply, "I'm twenty-nine."

My sisters and brother and I just stared at each other. Mama was so old, I just knew she was going to die soon! I ran into the front room, crawled under the high bed and cried and cried. My sisters and brother ran after me, and when I told them, "Mama is going to die soon!" they all began wailing too.

*A Memory
from Ruby*

*My mother was always so
unhappy. I've never seen an
unhappier woman. She didn't
really have fun till after she and
Papa moved to Phoenix and the
kids were all gone and the
grandkids were coming around.
That's when she started having
a little bit of fun.*

When Mama heard all the racket, she found us and made us come out from under the bed and tell her what was wrong. Sobbing, I told her what we thought. We seldom saw Mama laugh out loud, but this time she did. She assured us she was going to live a long time, and that twenty-nine wasn't really old since some mothers were sixty years old. Sixty! We stared at each other in disbelief! Could someone actually be sixty years old? That night we heard Mama tell Papa what happened, and Papa laughed a long time too.

This one time that Mama laughed stands out to me because when I picture Mama I see a sad face on her. Papa enjoyed life more than Mama did because Mama didn't have time to enjoy life until later. She worked hard day and night from childhood on, and that can take the joy out of life. Also, Mama had her share of sorrows.

Mama's father got tuberculosis three years after they came to Canada. He coughed and coughed, and finally died at home. Then, soon after Mama married, she faced another tragedy. Angie wasn't actually Papa and Mama's first child. A boy, Jack, had been born first.

When Jack was about nine months old, he got sick. Papa and Mama waited to take him to a doctor, as all poor farmers did, hoping he would get better the next day. But he didn't improve, so they finally braved the Canadian winter and took him in a horse and buggy to see a doctor. Mama laid him in between two feather pillows to keep him warm during the open buggy ride. When they arrived at the doctor's he was dead. It may have been the extreme cold, or he may have smothered between the pillows. Perhaps he was so

Front row: Mama's mother, Militza, holding baby Angie, Mama's brother Jim, Papa's sister Katherine and Mama. Back row: Papa, Mama's brother Mac and her brother Duke. This photograph was taken in early 1914, about a year before I was born. Mama's father had passed away the year before.

A Memory from Angie

My mother used to hang my Papa's lunch on my neck and send me out into the wheat field. I would walk a very long way through the high grain—taller than I was—carrying a flag so my father could see me and call to me. Imagine, sending me out in the field like that. If you think the Lord doesn't take care of you! He had His hand right on me. I used to stand there and gaze at snakes. There were all kinds of snakes. I was so accustomed to seeing them, I just enjoyed them and went on!

---

sick that he just died. What really happened to Jack, no one will ever know.

None of us children even found out about Jack until we were adults. People just didn't talk about hard things in those days. They avoided them and went on with life, as I still do today—as do those of my generation. I guess that's why there are a few different versions of how Jack died—no one found out for sure because we avoided asking about it.

Some of us heard that Papa and Mama bundled up one cold winter day to take the wagon ride to church. Mama wrapped Jack in pillows to keep him warm, but when they arrived at church, he was blue and cold.

Angie remembers hearing that when Papa and Mama were traveling in their horse and buggy, Jack just fell between two feather pillows and smothered. Years later Mama told Angie that she still wondered whether or not Jack could have been revived. But Papa built a little box and buried him right away. Mama was haunted for years with the thought that he might have been buried alive.

Papa yelled at Mama, "You smothered him." Poor Mama, to have been blamed for this accident! Even when Papa and Mama were in their eighties, I heard Papa accuse her yet. He was ignorant of the effect his words must have had on her.

Mama also worked hard on the farm in Canada. Claude remembers Mama talking about having to lift those 120-pound bags of wheat during harvest just as the men did. No wonder Mama hated farming. On top of that, she had to go back in the house and prepare their meals—and take care of all us kids. It was on the farm in Canada that Mama went through another sad experience.

Papa and Daka had just bought a farm near Qu'appelle, outside of Regina, and we moved there. They built a barn with a tool house attached, a shanty really. We lived in the shanty while they built our house. The animals were stabled in the barn on the other side of the wall from us.

One day Papa and Daka were in town buying lumber to build our new house. Somehow, the prairie next to our barn caught on fire. Mama says she remembers taking some ashes outside, so maybe that's how the fire started. It spread to the barn that was

A Memory from Mama

I was cutting the kids' hair. I smelled a fire, and I ran out. The fire was under the shanty and starting to burn and starting to crack. I pulled the kids out of that little shanty, and I put the feather pillow outside, and I put them all on top of that feather pillow. And I tried to go about half a block to get the water to stop the fire. How silly I was! And next to us in the stable was a horse, cow and a little calf. And I went in there to loosen them up. But the way they was tying that, I didn't know how to loosen them. That was easy, if I just pull certain things, it would open. But I didn't know what to pull. And it tried to crack under me, the fire was coming down on me, and my back was burned, and I couldn't do nothing. So I got out and I stood there and waited.

attached to the shanty we were living in. The way I recall it, Mama picked up Angie and Claude and me, wrapped us in the *dushek* and threw us out the window. We were scared, but when Mama tossed us out the window, we thought it was great fun, so we started playing out there.

The barn was on fire too. Poor Mama, she was helpless and frightened. I can still see Mama opening the barn door to try to let the animals out. But there was no one around to help. Even though I was only three years old, I still remember the dreadful sound of the horse screaming. The animals just burned to death.

A neighbor finally showed up, but the fire continued to burn across other people's farms and went all the way to the railroad before it stopped. Thank God for the railroad, Mama said. When Papa and Daka finally arrived home, everything was ashes.

I'm sure those experiences affected Mama. But regardless of what she went through, Mama still tried hard to do what was right. She was a dedicated mother and an obedient wife, stoic in her attitude. She was a sweet old-fashioned girl—that's what her pictures show—and a good mother, a wonderful mother. We learned many things from Mama—almost everything we know except what we learned from formal education.

Mama taught us girls how to iron. I ironed more beautifully than anybody else in the family, so I got to iron all of Papa's white shirts. I heated two heavy flatirons on the coal stove in the kitchen. I ironed with one until it cooled down, then I put it back on the stove and unlatched the small iron handle from it. The handle had a wooden grip so it wouldn't get hot, and I latched it onto the other flatiron that had been heating up. I did a beautiful job on Papa's shirts, and I was proud of it. But sometimes I scorched the shirts, and Mama had to wash them all over again!

Of course, Mama knew how to sew and knit and crochet. She knitted each of us a *chuke* with a tassel to wear on our heads in the winter. Mine was maroon and black, and it came down over my ears. Mama did beautiful embroidery and crochet work, though I can't imagine when she had time. She stiffened her crocheted lace by dipping it in sugar water, then letting it dry. She turned each piece over onto the wrong side and ironed it on a towel. That way it came out perfect.

A Memory from Ruby

When Mama's cooking and cleaning was done, sometimes she would crochet. She even crocheted curtains. And she crocheted pretty lace on all our panties, a little ruffle around the leg. At that time, you dolled up panties a little that way. She did her finer hand crocheting on those items.

A Memory from Angie

Mama taught us all to sew. We got to make our first skirts when we were seven. That was our first sewing lesson—just a plain little skirt with a band on it. We were very proud of it.

Mama thought that the only lovely thing for a girl to wear was a smocked dress. If she could smock one dress for each of her little girls, that was the ultimate. We each had a smocked dress, and she had a lot of little girls! She never slept, poor dear. She was always washing or ironing or sewing.

A Memory from Stella

If Mother got upset with one of us, and she could manage, she flicked us in the head with her thimble. Oh, man, that hurt!

When I was about eleven Mama told me that I had to learn how to crochet. "All girls have to learn to crochet," she said, and there was no discussion. Mama learned how to crochet when she was five. Dorothy says Mama even crocheted curtains at that age, but she loved it. Me—I hated it, but Mama made me do it anyway.

Mama sewed a small bag out of a scrap of material with a loop that fit over my arm. I kept my needles and thread and the pieces I practiced on in there. I still have that bag. I learned to crochet edging, but I cried all the time I was doing it. I would rather have read a book instead, but I didn't have the choice. Mama was so mad at me because I cried instead of listening and learning.

"Stop crying," Mama scolded me. "Listen to me, just listen to me. Here's all you have to do." She tried to teach me three or four steps at once instead of just the first step, then the second. What did she know about how to teach? If she had taught me one thing at a time—first put your needle here, then do this with your thread, then do this—maybe it would've been easier. Oh, I had a real hard time with it. I had no self-confidence, I guess. I was just sure I couldn't do it. It looked too complicated. I was lost.

After struggling with it for a while, I finally caught on a little bit and actually found it kind of interesting. But I would still rather have read a book!

On Chouteau Avenue Mama didn't have a lot of money to waste on making cookies and pastries. But later when we could afford it, she made lots of wonderful goodies. All of us—and anyone who ever visited our house—remember Mama for the delicious things she baked. Mama really enjoyed baking. Her greatest joy came from watching people enjoy the pastries she made. So many people remember her for her baking. Even today, people tell me which one of her pastries was their favorite.

Mama made a sweet yeast bread that we called *kolatcha*. She sprinkled sugar all over it, and it was so delicious! Sometimes she put jelly on it because that's all we had. Later on when we kids began working she could afford to spread apricots or nuts on it. She also made a leaflard cake with a nut filling that she called a pocketbook. Now nobody even knows what leaflard is. Her *leistichas* were made of a really delicate sweet dough that was rolled thin and fried, then dusted with powdered sugar. At Christmas she baked a few simple sugar cookies with nuts on the top.

Sometimes Mama made a poppy seed roll. The dough was rolled out and spread with poppy seed filling, then rolled up and baked. Once right after the poppy seed roll was taken out of the oven, we gathered around, waiting for a slice with our mouths watering. But when Mama started to cut it up, we found a roach baked inside! We all laughed because we knew he wouldn't crawl around our house anymore. But Mama didn't laugh. She threw up her hands and cried, "*Eyou! Eto sad.*" That's something like, "Well, what do you know! It finally happened."

But Mama is best remembered for her strudel. Friends and relatives who were treated to her strudel still comment about it to this day. It was as flaky and crisp as could be. She made the dough with a handful of this and a pinch of that, knowing just when it was perfect. Then she lifted the whole lump of dough in the air and spread it out with her fists, like pizza makers do. After she put it back on the table, she pulled at the edges, going around and around until the dough was spread from one side of the table to the other. It was so thin you could read a newspaper through it. Papa walked around the table, fanning the dough to dry it. Mama dabbed it with chunks of lard (later she used butter). Then she laid the filling in a line across the dough and rolled it up. She snaked the strudel around inside a baking pan. My, did that smell wonderful as it was baking!

Each of us had a favorite strudel filling. Mine was cheese—a sweet cottage cheese filling. I loved the raisin filling too. Mama made her own raisins by drying grapes in the sun. She also filled her strudel with apples and cherries and even pumpkin. There was never any strudel left over—never, never!

None of us learned how to make Mama's strudel exactly the way she did except Lee, Jimmy's wife. Jimmy and Lee lived with Papa and Mama in 1947 after Jimmy got out of the Navy. That's when Lee learned to make many of Mama's traditional dishes. We all learned to make some of Mama's delicious dishes, and we saw Mama make strudel so often that we just figured we knew how to do it. But we never sat down and learned as Lee did. Later Angie became the chef of the family, though, and she did a pretty good job of duplicating Mama's strudel.

After I grew up, moved away and had a family of my own, we sometimes drove to visit Papa and Mama. Every time we arrived, Mama had strudel and chicken soup ready for me. She always made me cheese and raisin strudel. And she knew how much I loved her homemade noodles in soup, so she always made extra soup for me, with those noodles she made by hand and cut up real tiny. Oh, I couldn't wait until we arrived because I knew we would have chicken soup with lots of noodles!

Mama wanted me to talk when I visited—talk about everything or anything. She wanted to know about everybody. I talked and ate at the same time, and Mama listened.

Mama showed her love by her actions. When I was about eleven, I had my tonsils taken out at City Hospital. Angie had hers taken out then too. When kids hit a certain age, it was the thing to do. I remember that the ward was full of crying children, probably all poor like me, receiving free medical care. I was crying too because my throat hurt so badly.

Mama was there, feeding me gelatin. "Don't cry," she soothed me. "You can come home soon." Her actions demonstrated her love.

Mama yelled at us, but we expected her to yell at us. We never thought about whether she loved us or not. Nobody ever talked about things like that as people do today. Of course she loved us—why, she took care of us, didn't she? No, we didn't ask, "Do you love me?" We didn't say, "Oh, I love you, Mama." And Mama didn't answer,

"*Ya volem tebe, Militza.*" No, we never talked like that. Later on as we all grew older, we sent cards to Mama with beautiful words on them, and she cried. We all knew we cared about each other, but nobody went around saying it.

Mama was a real Christian. She always told us to treat everybody right. She said the words. Parents today don't say the words, like, "Don't steal anything that doesn't belong to you" or "Don't tell lies." They assume their children automatically know right from wrong, and they don't. In those days mothers said the words and teachers said the words, and we learned from them.

Mama always told us how to act. We found out how to dress from watching other people, but Mama taught us how to be respectable young ladies. She never showered us

---

A Memory from Dorothy

Mother was really a smart woman. For all her lack of formal education, she was so intelligent. When I lived in Phoenix at the same time that she and Papa did, I saw how she treated Papa and the psychology she used. I asked her questions about when we were growing up and how she did this or that. "I just used common sense," she said. She had so much innate common sense and psychology. She raised us the way psychologists tell you to raise your kids today.

I told her, "Mom, you think you're not educated. You don't ever have to worry. You are so intelligent." I wanted her to know how much I appreciated her and loved her, and I told her all the time. I wanted her to hear something good about herself because she was so wonderful.

Mama and with her mother, Militza,
whom we called Mika, in about 1932.
I was named after her, but later I
decided I wanted to be called Millicent.

with compliments, but she was proud of us.

I learned how to sew and iron and bake from Mama—and how to bind a rag around my chest to hold my bosom in! But what I really learned from Mama was her generosity and kindness toward others. She took food to people who were sick, even when we didn't have enough to share. And Mama was always available for any of her church people who needed help.

From Mama's example I also learned how to treat my parents. Every single Sunday night Mama wrote to her mother in Canada. Each week when she sat down with pen and paper in hand we kids danced around her sing-songing, "*Slatka moya mati! Slatka moya mati! Slatka moya mati!*" That was how she started every letter: "My sweet mother." And all of us kids treated Mama and Papa wonderfully as they got older. We couldn't do enough for them. We bought things for Mama and showed her how much we loved her, trying to fill in the void. And in many cases, we succeeded.

Papa was arrogant and thought he was always right, and Mama bore up under his dominance. We could see when we were growing up that Mama had more common sense than Papa. She could figure things out and knew how things would turn out if this or that happened. But Papa overruled her and said, "No, this is what I want to do." He had to have his way. He believed it was a man's prerogative to dominate and even to lose his temper. He was a stubborn Serb, that's what he was.

When Angie was a young woman, she had a Serbian boyfriend. He came to pick her up while she was still upstairs getting ready. Mama met him at the door. When she saw him, she asked, "Are you Serbian?" He very proudly answered yes, thinking that would please Mama.

"You go away and you never come back," Mama told him. "I don't want any of my girls to go out with Serbian men!" And she closed the door in his face.

When Angie came downstairs, she asked where her boyfriend was. Mama told Angie, "He's gone away and he's not coming back. I don't want any of you girls to marry a Serbian man." Angie was mad, and she ran back upstairs and cried. But Mama had her way.

We knew how difficult it was for Mama, always trying to make up for Papa's shortcomings. Still, we were all in for a shock at Papa and Mama's fiftieth wedding anniversary. Family members came from all over the country to celebrate their golden anniversary with

Stella, Dorothy, Millie, Claude, Bee Bee, Ruby and Angie, with Mama and Papa at their fiftieth anniversary party in 1961. Jimmy couldn't make it.

My lovely Mama on the right, with her girlfriend, Fika. They're both about seventeen, dressed beautifully with their old-fashioned hats and clothes.

Papa and Mama. We gave them a banquet at the Safari Hotel in Scottsdale, Arizona, in 1961. Everyone was sitting around the banquet table, dressed in their best. Papa and Mama were in the center, and we grown-up children were sitting around them with our families. One of the grandkids said to Mama, "Tell us something about how you and Grandpa met fifty years ago."

"Well," responded Mama slowly as she stood up, "My mother told me I had to marry Artur. I told my mother I didn't want to marry Artur, and I told him I wasn't ready to marry. My mother said, 'He's a nice man, he's a good boy, he goes to the church, he's Serbian, and his family has a farm.' She said I would have a good life."

Mama explained how everyone kept persuading her, so she finally agreed to marry Papa. "I didn't want to marry him, and my Mama said I had to. I told my mother, 'You're going to be sorry,' and she was."

Then Mama sat back down. We were all stunned. Poor Papa just hung his head. Mama didn't even realize she had said anything that hurt him.

Though Mama agreed to marry Papa, some girls refused their parents' choice of a husband for them. In Canada Mama had a best girlfriend from the laundry whose name was Fika. She was a pretty little thing, only about up to Mama's chest. But when Fika's mother picked out the man for her to marry, she refused. Instead Fika jumped in the river and drowned herself.

Mama's mother, Militza, did come to see her error in judgment about Papa. About fifteen years after Papa and Mama married, Papa got into some kind of trouble and was away from home for a while. Mama's mother (we called her *Mika*, which was our way of saying "Grandma" in Serbian) came to St. Louis for a while to help Mama with her seven children. Mika liked Papa before she came to visit, even though she had lost money investing in his ideas. He was always personable and friendly to her. But when she saw how poor we were and how hard Mama worked, she walked through our house, throwing her arms into the air, saying, "*Eyou! Bozhe moya!* Moda, I'm so sorry I made you marry him. It's all my fault."

As the years went by, Papa had more contact with the world around him and with different kinds of people, and he changed, though not completely. He still felt that being the dominating father and husband was the way it should be. But he did become a lot better. He brought the coal and wood upstairs and did the things men do in a family, but I'm not sure he ever learned to appreciate Mama.

Mama always combed her long dark brown hair straight back and wound it up into a braided knot at the back of her neck, which she kept in place with large wire hairpins. Of

A Memory from Stella

When Pop came to the States, he got his naturalization papers. That made all the children who were born in Canada naturalized Americans. But Pop didn't think anything about Mother.
Well, 1941 comes along and Mother is still an alien, after living in the States since 1920. That's when they interned the Japanese, and all the aliens had to register. We thought she was going to be sent back to Canada. She had to study for three years and take the citizenship test. That's when she started writing in English instead of Cyrillic. It wasn't very good handwriting, like a six-year-old's. But she learned a little. That's typically old world. The father does for himself and the kids—forget about the wife.

course, Mama always wore a long dress, even when she was washing clothes or cooking or scrubbing floors for someone else. Women didn't wear slacks in those days. Once in the thirties when my sisters and I were downtown, we saw a mannequin modeled after Marlene Dietrich in the window of Famous-Barr Department Store. The mannequin was wearing slacks. How Marlene Dietrich shocked the feminine world by introducing slacks for women! She created quite a sensation all over the world. We all looked at the mannequin and said to each other, "I would never want to look like that." Now we all wear slacks. But not Mama—she never wore anything except a dress until the day she died.

After Mama quit working and we had moved to another house, every day before Papa came home she went upstairs and cleaned up and combed her hair and put on a crisp dress. I'll always remember that, but I don't think Papa even noticed or cared. He just carried on as usual.

Sometimes Papa and Mama yelled at each other. Most of the time Papa yelled at Mama. Then she didn't say much. She didn't yell back too often. Once on a cold wintry Sunday afternoon, though, I saw something really strange. We were all just sitting around the wood stove in the middle of the front room. Papa and Mama were sitting on the davenette, and I saw Papa hug Mama, actually put his arm around her. I had never seen him do that before.

We were sure Mama cared about Papa, even though they had many disagreements and lots of financial problems. Papa and Mama married for life—problems or no problems. Once Mama married, she gave her whole heart to it. Why, once we even saw Mama defend Papa when it was obvious he was wrong. She came to his aid, and we kids were so surprised!

Though their marriage had problems, it lasted sixty-eight years. Everyone had problems, but people never thought of leaving each other. Papa and Mama raised a family together, and family was everything. Mama was committed to Papa, and she stayed by his side all her life. In fact, when Papa died in 1979, Mama said, "My work is finished. I know the Lord will take me now." And she was right. Within a month, she too left earth for her much deserved reward.

But when I was a child at 2943 Chouteau Avenue, I didn't think about what Mama went through or how hard she worked or whether or not she loved me. All I thought of was playing and going to school.

Chapter Seven

Chouteau School Days

I have always been a curious person with a great desire to learn new things. To me, a good education is life's great accomplishment. Without it, I knew I wouldn't get anywhere. I felt so proud to be able to go to Chouteau School and start learning along with the other children. It was a real privilege to me.

Still, I had a hard time getting up for school on cold winter mornings. We four girls nestled under the *dushek*, real warm, until we heard Papa making a fire in the stove in our room. Papa rattled a little lever to shake the ashes into the pan, and what a racket that made! He made no effort to be quiet. Then he took the pan outside and emptied it in the ash pit. On his way back in he brought some wood and dropped it on the floor.

When I heard the commotion, I snuggled under the *dushek* some more, thinking, *Oh, if I stay under here longer, maybe when I get out it'll be warm.* Even now I hate the cold. I have a fear of being cold, and I find myself even today buying more sweaters than I need. I love having enough firewood stacked up outside. It makes me feel rich, knowing I'll be warm all winter.

We had two stoves—the cook stove in the kitchen and the wood stove in the front room. The wood stove was round and tall, with lots of shiny chrome trim. Now people look at those old wood stoves and think, *Wow, weren't they beautiful!* But in those days everybody had stoves like that, and they were a chore to handle. In the summer Papa took ours apart and stored it on the porch to give us more space in the front room.

But in the winter our house was so cold in the mornings that we could see our breath when we peeked out from underneath the *dushek.* Actually, it was almost worse on spring and autumn days because Papa would say optimistically, "Oh, the sun's going to shine later. We don't have to make a fire today." So when we really needed heat the most—when we were getting out of our warm cozy beds—we shivered instead.

It's no wonder we kids had head colds most of the time. The front room windows got light frost all over the inside so we couldn't see out. But the window in the kitchen didn't frost up because that cook stove was used constantly all year long. Before we went to bed Papa stoked the kitchen stove. I guess he woke up in the middle of the night to add wood, but those are things kids don't notice. In the morning he threw in some more wood. So when we were called to get some clothes on to go to school, we dashed into the kitchen and dressed next to that big cook stove.

Because we didn't have a closet, Mama kept our clothes in the kitchen, in one of the two *orman*s. They were dark and varnished and had lots of drawers. In the kitchen, we put on our best clothes for school. If a girl had a beautiful dress, she wore it to school. Little boys wore suits if they had any, knickers with ties and shirts. There were no such things as jeans or T-shirts. We took care of any nice clothes we had. When we came home from school, we changed from our good clothes into our play clothes right away.

After we dressed we all sat down together to eat breakfast. Papa said a short prayer, and Mama served us bread in coffee with a little milk. Occasionally she put sugar in it. Mama made coffee from the used grounds Mr. Caram gave us from his restaurant, and the delicious smell of the coffee helped warm us. Sometimes we ate *tarana* with a little sugar on top. Then Mama gave each of us two slices of bread to take to school for lunch.

When we finished eating, we ran the four or five blocks up Montrose Avenue to Chouteau School. We weren't cold anymore because we were moving. We never sat still except in class. Since Angie was the oldest she got to carry the bottle of homemade ketchup to school. At lunch time we all stayed in our class-rooms and ate. Angie went from room to room, putting catsup on our large slices of bread. Dorothy said Angie never put enough catsup on her bread. Some days we had jelly on our bread, but I never remember having meat in a sandwich while we were at Chouteau School.

When a friend at recess had something good to eat, like an apple or a piece of cake, those of us who didn't have anything asked, "Can I have a bite?" or when it was candy, "Can I have a suck?" If we were denied, we circled around our friend chanting, "Stingy guts, stingy guts, stingy guts." Sometimes it worked, and we got a piece. Sometimes she ran away. If someone was eating an apple, the first kid who yelled "cores" got the leftover apple core. An apple core was a real treat!

When we first started going to school in America, we didn't speak much English. But

---

A Memory from Ruby

About the only time we had milk was when we had tarana. *We never had milk to drink because it was too expensive. We had coffee occasionally, a kind of watered-down coffee. In school when the teacher asked, "Have you had your milk today?" I raised my hand yes because I had a little bit of milk in my coffee!*

A Memory from Angie

When Millie and Claude and I started school in America, we spoke mostly Serbian. The little English we knew we spoke with a British accent, as they spoke in Canada and Europe. So they put us all in kindergarten—no matter our ages—because they couldn't understand us. They told Mother that we had to speak English at home, and if we didn't, we'd all have to stay in kindergarten. That upset my mother, and she worked really hard at trying to speak English and having us do the same.

it wasn't so bad because many other children—Romanians, Hungarians and Croatians—didn't know much English either. So we all picked up words from each other and from the teachers. I don't remember it being a hardship.

Papa knew English, but Mama didn't know much when we came to America. Papa and Mama were so proud to be Americans, and they wanted to assimilate right away—to do everything right, to look and act like Americans. Mama wanted to learn English, and she insisted that we teach her words at night. Mama said, "Now, let's not speak Serbian at home until we can all speak good English." I'm proud of my parents because they wanted to learn the American ways and they wanted to learn English. I wish all immigrants today came with the same attitude, but so many of them want to stay in their own groups and not learn the language. They don't want to join in and become what I call Americans.

Mama learned to speak pretty well, but she sounded like many Eastern Europeans did who learned English later in life. We all laughed at her cute ways of saying things. She was a great sport about it too, laughing at herself. Mama said that a sponge *observed* water. She said *winegar* for vinegar and *vater* for water. Years later when my youngest sister Bee Bee was going to have a baby, Mama asked her if she had a good *B.O.* Of course, she meant O.B. During World War II when Jimmy was in the Navy, Mama went to visit him in *Pepsi*

Cola, Florida, or so she said. She taught herself to read a little English, but she never wrote much in English, except to sign birthday cards "Mama," or later, "Grandma."

Papa knew English quite well, but he made some typically foreign mistakes. As we kids learned proper English, we corrected Papa and told him he should talk better. When we pointed out an error, his pride flared up and he said in Serbian, "*Izish tvoyi guzitza.*" That meant something like "eat your butt" or "kiss your ass." Later he taught my baby sister Bee Bee to say that to Mama just to annoy her, and it worked. Mama always scolded him when he talked like that. Papa was sometimes uncouth, but he had a little boy kind of charm about him.

In school I was a talker. I gabbed with the kids in front of me and behind me. Once in the third grade my teacher had to tell me to be quiet several times. We were quite fearful and respectful of teachers then, but I guess I just didn't want to stop talking. After her patience with me wore out, she asked me come up to her desk. In front of the whole class she taped my mouth shut!

I was really embarrassed, and I started to cry. When recess came, she still hadn't taken the tape off my mouth. I had a cold, so I couldn't breathe through my nose, and my crying only made it worse. I had such a hard time breathing that it scared me, so I cried more. I was terrified, but I wouldn't dare take the tape off myself. That would be disobeying my teacher.

Claude was in my class at that time, and he finally told the teacher that I couldn't breathe. So she pulled the tape off all at once, and boy did that hurt. But at least I could breathe again. I don't know whether that experience kept me from talking in class again or not, but it probably helped for a while.

We often had colds in the winter, but we didn't realize it because they were so commonplace. We suffered from earaches and fevers too. In fact, I had earache after earache. The pus ran from my ear down my neck. In those days people didn't call for a doctor to come to the house unless it was a real emergency—at least, the people we knew didn't. Who could afford it? You delivered your own babies and nursed your own sicknesses. Doctors were for life-and-death situations—or for the rich. But I guess a screaming child

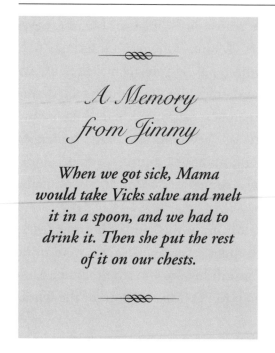

A Memory from Jimmy

When we got sick, Mama would take Vicks salve and melt it in a spoon, and we had to drink it. Then she put the rest of it on our chests.

with a constant earache was too much for Mama and Papa. They finally called for the doctor.

After looking into my infected ear, the doctor inserted an instrument and pulled out, of all things, a kernel of wheat! Later I remembered a time on the farm in Canada when wheat was piled high in the new barn Papa and Daka built after the fire. The building smelled of new wood, a wonderful smell to me. Angie and I played in the wheat just as children play in a sandbox. We rolled around in it and put it in our noses and in our ears. It was great fun! One of those kernels of wheat must have been stuck in my ear for years, causing infection after infection!

Once on Chouteau Avenue when I was really sick, Mama made a mustard plaster, put it on my chest and wrapped a rag around it. I don't know what that did, but it sure was a mess for Mama to clean up. Sometimes she gave us a tiny bit of Serbian whiskey called *rakiya* in hot water with a little sugar to break up a cold.

The school nurse provided a lot of the medical care for children then. If we were sick at school or complained of a fever or threw up, she sent home a note telling Mama what she should do for us and how long we should stay out of school.

Every Friday the teachers examined our heads to see if we had lice. If one sent a note home with us announcing our tiny visitors, Mama bought a gallon of coal oil. She made us dip our heads in the coal oil. Mama told us to keep our eyes shut, but oh, I'm sure we got some of it in our eyes. How dangerous that was, but that's the way everyone rid themselves of lice then. Seems like most of the kids on the block got those notes too.

Miss Greer, my fifth grade teacher, was tall and skinny and had red, red hair. She was single, as all the women teachers were. Married women were not allowed to teach then, not anywhere in St. Louis. Miss Greer was from New York, or as she pronounced it, "New *Yoik*."

One day we had a spelling test. Miss Greer read the first word: *woik*. We all looked at each other, as we had never heard that word before. But since we had been taught to spell the word by the way it sounded, many of us wrote w-o-i-k. Of course, when we got our papers back, *woik* was marked wrong. Most of the class missed it, and she must have realized why, although she never mentioned it. After that she spelled out w-o-r-k on the blackboard when she said it. I don't think we ever caught on to her way of pronouncing words! We all liked her, though, because she was pretty and very nice to us.

A Memory from Angie

I had a teacher in the fourth or fifth grade who was so cruel. She kept me after school all the time and just made me sit. She terrified me so badly scolding me. She would pound on the desk with each word as she asked slowly and deliberately, "What did I say that was?" When she did that, I couldn't remember anything, I was so terrified. She made me write with my right hand, even though I'm left-handed. Today, I write with my right hand, and I do everything else with my left hand.

Mama went to school one day and walked into the room and caught that teacher pounding on my desk, yelling at me. She really laid that teacher out. I don't remember what she said to her, but she really gave it to her. I think Mama must have had me taken out of that teacher's class because I don't remember being with her anymore after that.

A Memory from Ruby

We had strict teachers. They were good. We learned so fast it wasn't funny. My education through high school was worth a college education anytime. When I talk to college-educated kids now, as far as I can see, all they get out of college is the fun of meeting people. Most of the kids don't really study in college. The subjects they should have taken in high school, now they take in college. And all the electives available now—the only electives we had were readin', writin' and 'rithmetic!

The teachers at Chouteau School were strict, and our principal, Miss Proctor, was someone to be feared. If you were sent to her office, she turned you over and spanked your bottom or she hit your hands with a ruler. Claude says that if you were mean, she took you in her office and turned you around and hit you on the back of your legs with a switch—and it hurt! I guess he would know. They beat kids in those days. It may not have been the best thing to do, but we sure minded.

But we had some nice teachers too, like Mr. Pincus, my science teacher in the sixth grade. We had to dissect a roach in his class, and everyone was supposed to bring a big roach to school. One boy said he didn't know where to get one. So I raised my hand and shook it furiously until Mr. Pincus finally called on me. Then I announced proudly, "Mr. Pincus, I can bring a lot of roaches—enough for everybody!"

When I went home, my sisters and brothers helped me collect roaches. Some of them we caught live. The ones we had to kill, we stepped on lightly so we didn't smash them.

I was so glad to bring the roaches to school to help the other kids. All the kids who needed roaches thanked me. I was sad that they didn't have any roaches.

Once when my teacher was talking about the beautiful clouds in the sky, I raised my hand. "What is it?" she asked. I said proudly, "I've got a brother named Cloud." So that's a big joke in our family now. When I see Claude, I ask, "Are you my brother Cloud?"

One year I was held back. I found myself in my brother Claude's class, and he didn't like it at all. But I was only there for half a year, then they moved me up. I don't know why I had to do the grade over. Maybe it was because Angie and I had to take turns staying home to watch baby Stella while Mama was working, and I missed too much school. Maybe I failed a subject, probably arithmetic. I liked all my classes except arithmetic. I never could learn to add the way Miss Meyer taught. I was always scared to go into her class, and I cried when she called on me and I didn't know the answer. At night

A Memory from Claude

I was five years old when I started kindergarten at Chouteau School. On the first day, the teacher asked, "What is your name?"

I said, "Vlada."

"What?" she asked.

"Vlada," I repeated.

"Oh, we can't pronounce that," she said. "We're going to call you Claude."

So I went home and told Mom, "They can't pronounce my name at school. They're going to call me Claude." And Mom says, "Okay." She said okay because we foreigners would comply with anything the Americans asked of us because we thought that was the right thing to do. So my name became Claude.

———∞———

A Memory from Angie

*In 1927 there was a tornado. We were in class on the third floor
at McKinley School. The teacher made us stand up against the wall,
and the roof blew off. It was so scary, I can relive it right now.*

A Memory from Claude

*In 1927 we had a tornado. In those days they didn't put the
kids in the basement. So we went to the window at Chouteau School
and looked out and saw the tornado go right by on Grand Avenue.
The teachers showed us the tornado as it went by!*

A Memory from Ruby

*I don't remember the tornado at school, so it must not have hit my
school. But Papa wanted to see the tornado damage, and no one wanted to
go with him but me. We went on the streetcar to see the area that really got
hit by the tornado. It was mainly two-story houses, and all the fronts and
roofs were blown off. We stood there and moaned at how terrible it was.
We saw the women walking around in the upstairs, crying.*

———∞———

in bed I knew I had to go to her class again the next day, and the thought would scare me, so I cried. Even today I shy away from numbers.

One day soon after we moved to 2943 Chouteau Avenue, when we were the poorest we ever were, the teachers sent home a note saying that the George Washington birthday celebration in the schoolyard was coming up. Would Mama please send five cents for each child for American flags?

Mama panicked when we read the note to her. She didn't have the money, and she didn't know what to do. Three children in school meant that she needed fifteen cents. So she asked Angie to write a letter to the teachers saying that our Mama didn't have the money, but if the teachers would trust Mama and give us the flags anyway, she would send whatever she could every week. So we took that note to the teachers. After they read the note, they told us to tell Mama that they would let us have the flags, as she asked. Then Mama started sending money in, three cents one week, four cents another, two cents the next—whatever she could manage.

After several weeks, when Mama had paid the fifteen cents, the teachers told us to tell Mama they were coming to visit. They wanted to meet a family that was so honest and conscientious. Mama was so thrilled that she put on a clean dress and placed a white tablecloth on the kitchen table. She served the peaches that she canned and *kolatcha*, the sweet bread she made. When the teachers came, she sat down and talked with them in the best English she could manage. We were proud that Mama could carry on a conversation like our very smart teachers. We proudly told all the kids at school that the teachers had come to visit us at our house.

When I finished sixth grade, it was time to move on to McKinley School to attend seventh and eighth grades. All summer long I was scared, realizing that I had to go to that big school. Would I know where to go? Would I find my room? Well, it turned out all right after all that worrying. At McKinley I made many new friends. That's where my girlfriends and I chanted, "I don't smoke and I don't chew, and I don't go with boys who do." But before I left Chouteau School, I had all my friends write in an autograph book. This is what they wrote, in their own words—right or wrong.

In your golden chain of friendship, regard me as a link. Adele Bauer

When you are old and cannot see, put on your specs and think of me. Edward Linhart

When you get married and live upstairs, don't come down and borrow my chairs. Your Friend, Theresa Seith

1/25/29 In after years, when this you see, I wonder what your name will be. As Every, Bunny Gallagher

1/24/28 Love many Trust few and always paddle your own canoe. Bee Bee Caram

When you get married and your husband get cross, Show him the broom and tell him "I'm Boss." Boots Schlivfste

Dear little girl, I hope you dont feel hurt if your husand wont buy you a nice little skirt. Jack Schulz

Roses are red, violets are blue, my feet stink and so do you. Yours until grasss grows on Pacific Ocean. Shorty

What shall I write? What shall it be? Just these two words Remember Me. Your until the mountian peaks peeks. Corinne Maness

When you get married and live by the lake please give me some of your wedding cake. Yours, Mary Papaovac

When you are old and cannot wiggle, think of me and you we'll giggle. Yours till Niagra Falls and the kitchen sinks. Virginia Ratican

Kiss you once kiss you twice kiss you three time you'll be my wive. Mary Martin

When you get married and live on a hill, Send my a kiss by the whip-por-will. Your pal, Velma Dudley.

I love you once, I love you twice. I love you better then a chinman loves rice. Wrote on Feb. 2, 1928. Thelma Watson 2941 Chouteau Ave Phone Grand 7686

6/15/28 Millie now, Millie ever, Petrov now but not forever. Your friend, Bernice Hardin.

When you get married and have some twins you can come down and borrow my safety pins. Your chum, Jennie Mertz

Red white and yellow. So your the girl who sole my fellow. Marie Gaffron.

I wish you luck, I wish you joy. I wish you first a baby boy. And when its hair begins to curl I wish you then a baby girl. Your's till the Princess slips, Elma Leslie.

Down in a valley carved on a rock Three little words forget-me-not. Yours until rubber tires. Olga Majtas

Jan. 25, 1929 When in this book you look When in this book you frown Remember the one that spoiled your book by writing upside down. Yours till Bed Springs. Clotilda DePalma

Jan 25 1929 Rosses are red Violets are blue Just three words I love You. Yours untill Hell freezes over and little divils go ice skating. Etheline Terry

June 3, 1931 When you get married, and live by the sea where the great brids fly, Stop one of them and sent me your best lullaby. Mary Harper age. 10.

I love you little I love you mighty I wish your pajamas was next to my nighties Don't get mistaken are either mislead I mean on my clothes line and not in my bed. Your friend, Annabell Knowles

Silver shines and so does tin. How I love you it is a sin. Your friend, Bessie Milosivich

1/25/29 When you are setting on your grandfathers knee spit on the floor and think of me. Edwena Huff

Jan 25, 1929 As sure as the vine growes around the stump, you are my little sugar lump. Your friend and school mate, Billy McCormick

Yours until hot dogs bark. Your sis, Ruby.

One day Papa was invited to attend a Patrons' Association meeting at Chouteau School. That was a group of parents interested in their children's school and activities, like the PTA of today. He was very proud to be asked. With his charm, in time he became its president.

After Papa had been attending the Patrons' Association meetings for quite a while, one of the mothers on the block asked Mama why she didn't go to the meetings. Why, she didn't realize that she could! I guess Papa never invited her. So she started attending and had a great time with the other mothers.

I'm sure Papa worked on quite a few projects through the Patrons' Association, but the important one to us kids was the annual Chouteau School picnic. The greatest adventure of my childhood years was going to Forest Park Highlands for the Chouteau School picnic. We lived for and dreamed about that day. Our annual school picnic was the most joyous time of our young lives!

Papa and the other members of the Patrons' Association went around to the neighborhood stores and got donations for the prizes to be given out to the school kids. I have the program for the 1929 picnic, and that year some businesses donated two dollars, some one dollar, others fifty cents or even twenty-five cents. A couple of businesses donated ten dollars each, and that was almost a fortune.

Prizes were donated for the races, including,

- a haircut, donated by Jake's Barber Shop
- one pair of Keds, donated by A. Cohn Shoe Store
- a baseball bat, donated by May's Hardware
- a pair of rubber heels, donated by Hoffman's Shoe Repair
- one box of handkerchiefs, donated by Bumstead's Dry Goods Company
- a 50-cent box of cookies, donated by J. H. Fleming
- one ring, donated by A. Malone Jewelry Store

Papa even donated some of the Rock-a-by Dolls he made at his doll factory.

The 1929 Chouteau School picnic program with a photograph of my beloved Chouteau School. It was built at 1306 South Ewing Avenue in 1894 and demolished in 1988. While it was being torn down, I went to see it. I ran to where men were working and grabbed one of the bricks to keep forever. I still have it.

TWENTY-SECOND ANNUAL PICNIC
Given by
CHOUTEAU SCHOOL
Mothers' Club and Patrons' Assn.

Forest Park Highlands
Monday, June 3, 1929

LINE OF MARCH

Will start at 9:00 A. M. sharp—From School north on Ewing Avenue, east to Chouteau Avenue, east to Jefferson, south on Jefferson to Park, west on Park to Montrose Avenue, cars will be waiting at 9:45 A. M., at Montrose and Park Avenues. Return cars will leave Park at 7:00 P. M.

174

We counted the days until the picnic came, and we couldn't sleep the night before such a wonderful day. When it finally arrived, we were delirious with joy!

The festivities began at nine in the morning. All the families and businesses on Park, Ewing, Chouteau, Jefferson and Montrose watched as the parade of schoolchildren, officials, teachers, bands and banners marched by. As Angie and I marched along, we were sure everyone noticed our shiny new socks—my orange socks (one slightly faded from being in Mr. Bumstead's store window) and Angie's red ones!

The parade in 1927 took on a special meaning. The name "Charles Lindbergh" was on everyone's tongue. He was a St. Louis hero. We were all jubilant when Lindbergh flew across the Atlantic. It was as if the Cardinals had won the World Series. Everybody was talking about this great feat—and St. Louis was a vital part of it. He was our native son. We were all so proud of him and the name he had chosen for his airplane. When Lindbergh came to St. Louis during the celebrations after his flight, all the schoolchildren went down to the wharf together in streetcars. We were all given American flags. When Lindbergh flew over us, we all waved our flags at him. He tipped his wings at us, and we were ecstatic!

After Lindbergh's flight Papa immediately started building a wooden *Spirit of St. Louis* airplane for Claude to carry in the Chouteau School parade. Papa painted it silver with the words in black which forever made our city famous: *Spirit of St. Louis*. Papa had always made wooden toys for the youngest ones in our family. I remember a little wooden car that we "drove" with our feet at the bottom. He also made a little tricycle out of wood.

But this *Spirit of St. Louis* airplane was really something—quite large, about four feet long and three feet wide. It wasn't made of a lightweight wood like balsa. It was big and heavy. Claude had a difficult time carrying it in the parade alone, so Papa helped him. How proud Claude was as he held the replica *Spirit of St. Louis* up high so everyone could see it! And see it they did, for when he marched by, all the bystanders clapped and cheered. That made Claude and Papa feel so important!

When the parade ended, we all boarded special streetcars with banners on the sides

---

A Memory from Dorothy

The school would have a picnic once a year at the Forest Park Highlands. That was one thing that Mother loved, and she would go to it. We would all take our picnic lunch, and everybody would go. Papa got Mama to go on those little dodg'em cars—those bumper cars. She got in one, and Papa got in one, and they bumped each other. Mama was dying laughing and having so much fun. It was really, really remarkable! And Papa was laughing and laughing at her. Mother never learned how to drive, but she turned the wheel on the bumper cars. Everybody bumped into her, and Papa bumped into her on purpose. She enjoyed that so much. Mother really never got to enjoy herself. She was always working. It made me so happy to see my mother so happy. We were little then.

---

that said, "Chouteau School Picnic." Each streetcar was crammed with laughing, screaming students who could scarcely believe this great day had finally arrived! When we got to Forest Park, we jumped off the streetcars and joined our parents.

Forest Park Highlands was like a carnival then, an amusement park with a Ferris wheel and a tall wooden roller coaster named the Mountain Ride. Stella says Papa received books of free tickets to all the rides because of his position with the Patrons' Association. People knew this and came up to him asking, "Mr. Petrov, do you have any free tickets?" So he proudly gave them out to everyone, as he was supposed to do as president.

We too went on all the rides with the free tickets. We loved the fun house, with those mirrors that made us look short and fat or tall and skinny when we stood in front of them. How we laughed! Dorothy walked through the "turning barrel" at the fun house too soon after two glasses of Mama's lemonade, and she threw up all over her dress. Jimmy rode the flying airplanes the most. The propellers turned, and to him it was like flying in an open cockpit.

Our whole family at Forest Park for the Chouteau School picnic. I'm on the left in my rayon socks, then Mama, Angie, Papa and Claude. Stella and Jimmy are in front, with Dorothy and Ruby kneeling behind them.

In between rides on the Racer Dip, a small roller coaster, and all the laughter of the fun house, we came back to our spot on the grass to eat the lunch Mama made. In our picnic basket were sandwiches—and sometimes even bananas! We washed it all down with real homemade lemonade!

Next came the footraces. Every grade had a footrace, each with its own prize. We all raced in our dresses and nice shoes—whatever we were wearing. The girls and boys raced separately. When it was my turn to race, Papa carefully instructed me, "Remember, the first prize is a pair of shoes from Bumstead's. Now you run fast so you can get those shoes." But I had read in the program that the second prize was a gallon of ice cream, and I decided to win the ice cream instead. I knew what I was going to do, no matter what Papa said.

The race began, and everybody screamed and cheered us on. I was ahead, but I slowed down so I could come in second. It must have been pretty obvious, because Papa sure was mad that I didn't win those shoes. But I knew he wouldn't hit me in front of all those people. It was grand for me because I received a coupon for a gallon of ice cream that we could redeem at Pevely Dairy, which was about five blocks away. So one evening soon after our school picnic Papa went to the dairy and brought home that prized gallon of ice cream.

We had to eat the ice cream right away because freezers weren't out yet. Our icebox kept things somewhat cool, but it wouldn't keep ice cream frozen. So we invited the Watsons over from next door—Thelma Watson and her mother and father and grand-mother. A couple of Palazzolo kids and some other friends came too to enjoy this fabu-lous treat. I hated sharing my prize with anybody—even my brothers and sisters—but in my heart I knew that I couldn't eat that much ice cream all by myself before it melted.

Eating the ice cream several days after the picnic seemed to make that glorious day last a little longer. It was never long enough for me.

Chapter Eight

At Play on the Block

Every day when we kids woke up, all we could think about was playing outside on the block. It was a joyous feeling. It seems that kids today don't play outside as we did. Of course, there were no other forms of entertainment—no computers or televisions to keep us inside. Every family on the block knew every other family, and all the mothers knew whose children belonged to which parents. The parents sat out at night on their stoops and talked to each other and laughed while we children played around them.

Papa sat around with the men in the evening, and they talked about Babe Ruth and

Jack Dempsey. Every boy wanted to be a boxer like Jack Dempsey. When he was fighting Gene Tunney, all the men wished they could have been there watching. But we girls had our heroes too. Helen Wills was a tennis champ, and all the women and girls were proud of her and so happy that a woman was a champion. But her life was a far cry from the lives of the mothers on Chouteau Avenue, who sat around at dusk and talked about their children and exchanged recipes. That was their enjoyment.

And, of course, there were the Cardinals. People in St. Louis were crazy over the Cardinals. We were all proud of them—they were our boys. Even the women and children followed their games. And every little boy who played baseball in the park wanted to be a champion like Babe Ruth—the king of the swats, as they called him—even if he wasn't a Cardinal.

A Memory from Claude

When I was ten, I sold papers at the corner of Chouteau Avenue and Jefferson. I was selling papers when the Cardinals beat the Yankees and won the series in 1926. They printed a special edition, an extra. I held the papers up and screamed, "Extra! Extra! Extra! Cardinals win the pennant!" I sold a lot of papers that day.

I remember the headlines, "Hornsby for President!" He was our manager. "Bottomly for Mayor!" He was the first baseman. People put signs up like that too. The town went crazy—absolutely wild. Everyone poured out into the streets. People tied refrigerators and stoves to the backs of their cars and pulled them down the streets, creating a great clatter. Pieces of metal and parts were left in the streets.

As we played and our parents sat and talked, sometimes a policeman rode by on a motorcycle with another policeman in the sidecar. They stopped and talked with our parents, and we gathered around to gaze at the sidecar. It was fascinating to us!

We played outside as long as we could get away with it at night, until the man came around and lit the gaslights on the street with a long pole. Then we kept on playing until our parents called us to come home. It was a glorious time in my life! But by nine o'clock the street was almost deserted. Everyone had gone to bed because everyone had to be up early. Plus, there was nothing else to do after it got dark.

Every morning in the summer we kids rushed to Buder Playground, six blocks from us. What a haven Buder Playground was! It was more than just a public playground. It was a true playland. We loved to swing real high on the circle swing—a tall metal pole with swings on chains hanging from the top of the pole. Each swing was just a metal bar about chin

A Memory from Ruby

We played on the circle swing at Buder Playground. It was made of metal pipe, a ten-sided circle on a big base. We hung on the edges and ran, then lifted our legs to swing around. I remember hitting my chin pretty badly. I must have had a fever at the same time, because that night I dreamed what I always dreamed when I had a fever: the dushek *was rolling toward me, coming to smother me. I still have that scar on my chin.*

height. Sometimes we sat on them, but mostly we just hung from them with our hands. We got a running start and swung so high, sailing through the air. Sometimes we hit the pole or banged into one another in mid-air. The instructor in charge would hurry over with mercurochrome and bandages to patch us up. Then up we went again! To me, this was more fun than anything else on the playground.

We stayed there all day, then reluctantly went home to eat a quick supper. In the

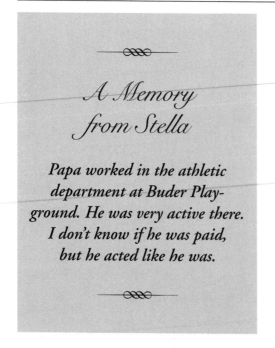

Papa worked in the athletic department at Buder Playground. He was very active there. I don't know if he was paid, but he acted like he was.

evening we raced back to the playground, and the teachers told us ghost stories. Oh, those always upset me, yet I kept going back. That's where I first heard Edgar Allan Poe's "The Raven." I was scared to death—too scared to walk home alone. I should never have listened to those ghost stories. They stuck in my mind, and I never could get them out. I don't think I would have been so afraid later in life if I hadn't heard those ghost stories.

During the day we learned arts and crafts from the teachers at Buder Playground. We made raffia and reed baskets. I sat at the edge of the swimming pool waiting for the reed to soften in the water so it would become pliable enough to weave. How I loved to make things with my hands!

All the little girls were taught to sew. We made potholders out of scraps of material, a different color on each side. We padded them with bits of old blankets to make them thick, then we edged them with bias tape, sewing it on by hand.

Once we each made a dress—all by hand. The teachers showed us how to cut the dress out and sew it together. The best thing was that we were allowed to pick out our own material. My choice was white dimity with narrow white satin stripes and tiny red roses with green leaves. Oh, how I loved that material. I can close my eyes now and picture it. I thought that was the most beautiful material I had ever seen in my life, and I couldn't wait until I could put my dress on. Perhaps that's where I got my taste for dainty old-fashioned roses. Decades later I wallpapered our bedroom—the wall and even the ceiling—with wallpaper that had rows of golden roses on it.

One Sunday that summer I finally got to wear my handmade dress. When I received a compliment on it, I proudly announced, "I made it all by myself by hand." I wore it as

A Memory from Angie

Dorothy was the loudest kid on the street no matter where we lived.
She played ball and yelled the loudest and bossed everybody. She was darling.
She was very lively. She could beat anybody.

A Memory from Dorothy

Nobody knows about corkball today. You could play with two people on a team—
a pitcher and a batter. That's why you could play it anywhere with four people. But it
helped if you had three people on a team—then you could have an outfielder. If you
made one strike, you were out. If the catcher caught the ball, you were out. It wasn't
easy to catch that little ball. If you foul-balled it, you weren't out. Your team got three
strikes, then your team was out. Maybe you got to bat once or twice. Four hits made a
run, but you didn't run because there were no bases. The bat was a broomstick. They
made special narrow sticks for it, but we couldn't afford one. The fun of it was that
we could play in a small space, and that corkball wouldn't break a window.

long as it fit, then I kept it in my special drawer. I'd love to have that dress today. I saved it for a long time, but I suppose it and the potholders and the baskets went the way of many old things. We probably used them for a while, then gave them away.

At the end of the summer, the teachers sponsored a show. All the fathers and mothers and families came to view everything their children had made during the summer. I counted all the items we Petrov kids had made, and it came to fifty-six! The teachers said, "Well, the Petrovs made the most, but then there's more of them." Oh, were we proud! When I saw that dimity dress with the little roses hanging there in the show, I was so scared. I thought to myself, *Oh, I hope somebody doesn't steal it while it stays here overnight.* I loved it so much. But the next day, there it was, hanging so proudly. How lucky I was that no one took it!

We were always playing outside games—always. We made them up or copied what we saw other kids do, playing hide-and-go-seek, hopscotch and I Spy. Since we were a big family, we always had enough players for a team. There were so many of us that we were never without playmates.

Papa played corkball with us in the yard and in the park. He was good with kids because he always wanted to play. We learned sportsmanship from Papa. He didn't get mad if he lost or if his team lost, and he had a lot of patience. He took the time to show kids how to play, even if one of them was a slow learner. He became the Troop Master for Boy Scout Troop 118 at Chouteau School in 1926.

Ruby remembers that Papa had the scout meetings in our small flat, and they were crowded and noisy, with all the marching he made the scouts do. Jimmy was five, and he

---

A Memory from Angie

Papa was always teaching the scouts to form pyramids and do other gymnastic poses. All the things he had the scouts do, he made us do as well. He always led us in doing exercises or calisthenics, just as he did his scouts. We had to learn the poses too. After we learned them, he wanted us to be in those poses every time he took a picture of us.

Papa on the left directing his scouts to form a pyramid.

Jimmy is on top, Dorothy and Ruby next, then Angie, Claude and Millie, and Stella is lying on the ground.

Papa leading us in exercises at the park.

My Uncle Jim, Mama's brother, who was an Olympic wrestler for Canada.

Claude boxing with little blonde Jimmy.

was so proud to be the troop mascot. He wore a little scout uniform. Anything the troop needed, he went to get. Papa directed the scouts to form human pyramids, with four or five on the bottom row, then three on top of them, then two on top of them. Papa put Jimmy on the very top because he was the littlest and so cute.

When Jimmy and Claude were young boys, Papa really wanted them to follow in the footsteps of our Uncle Jim, Mama's brother. Uncle Jim wrestled for Canada in three Olympics, winning the bronze medal in the bantamweight class in 1928 in Amsterdam. He and his team won the gold in the 1930 British Empire Games. Later he coached the Canadian Olympic wrestling team for years. He sent me a lovely scarf he bought for me in Rome while he was there at the 1960 Olympics. Uncle Jim was later inducted into Canada's Sports Hall of Fame.

Oh, we thought Uncle Jim was the cat's meow! We talked about

Uncle Jim a lot because we were all so impressed with him. And Uncle Jim thought Papa was so smart and so creative, especially since he was relatively uneducated. Papa could do no wrong in Uncle Jim's eyes. Papa took a picture of Jimmy and Claude boxing with their fists, and he sent it to Uncle Jim. I guess that was as close to wrestling as Papa could get.

When Ruby was ten years old the Kodak company gave a free camera to everybody whose birthday fell on May 28th because that was the date the Kodak company was formed. Since that was her birthday, she received a box camera. Oh, boy, we thought that was wonderful. Maybe that's the camera Papa used to take pictures of us now and then.

Photographers came around too and tried to talk people into having their pictures taken. Before we had a camera, one day a photographer showed

Here I am at age eight, proud as a peacock on the pony.

up with a pony. Kids in the city never got the chance to ride on a pony. Oh, I begged and begged Mama to let me sit on the pony for a picture. She didn't have the extra money, but I finally wore her down. She paid the huge sum of twenty-five cents, and I got my picture taken on the pony.

Often we went to play at the neighbors' houses. One summer day Stella, Ruby, Dorothy and I went over to play with Helen Vesich, a little friend whose Serbian family lived a couple of blocks down the street, on Mississippi and Park. Stella was little, under four. Helen led us up into the attic to show us how we could get out onto the roof from there. So we went out through an attic window and walked around on the roof.

The roof had a skylight window that opened, and a screen was lying across the opening. Over the skylight was a little roof that kept the rain from coming in when the window was open. Helen ducked under the little roof and jumped over the screen. I followed, then Dorothy, then Ruby. But Stella walked on the screen, and it gave way. She fell through the screen and down to the bottom floor, landing right in the washtub where Mrs. Vesich was washing clothes! She plopped right into the water, not even hitting the rim. The angels must have been watching over her.

Imagine how surprised Mrs. Vesich was when Stella fell into her arms in the washtub! She quickly pulled her out and dried her off. By that time, we had all run down the stairs to see what happened to Stella. When Mrs. Vesich saw her daughter Helen, she told her, "Go get me a glass of cold water, right away." When Helen brought the cold water back, her mother threw it all over Helen and yelled at her for playing on the roof! We ran home with Stella to tell Mama all about it. Mama clasped her hands together and looked heavenward with the words *"Bozhe moya!"* on her tongue. She didn't believe it was luck. She thanked God for His protection.

Speaking of Stella, she was the one in the family who was neglected because she was several years younger than the four of us older girls—Angie, me, Ruby and Dorothy. As young girls in our teens, the four of us did everything together. But Stella wasn't with us most of the time. A lot of Stella's life is a blank to me. I feel that we neglected her terribly because she was in the middle, but she doesn't think so. All of a sudden Stella grew up and got married!

When one of the houses on the street needed a new roof, what a big event that was! The workers came in a truck pulling a small tank full of boiling hot tar. Whoever saw it first ran around the neighborhood alerting the other kids of its arrival. "Hey, the tar man's here, the tar man's here." Then we all ran up and stood around as if we were just watching from a distance. What little street urchins we were!

When the workers went up on the roof, we all converged on the big tar tank and peeled the soft little pieces of tar off the edges and chewed on them. After a while we spit the tar out with the black juices. We liked the taste, yet we didn't want to swallow it. It was like chewing gum. I still like the smell of tar today.

The iceman drove by every day with his horse and wagon. We loved it when the iceman came, especially in the summer. He looked up at our front window where Mama put the ice sign. It was a perfectly square piece of cardboard, and on each side was a different number that told the ice man how many pounds of ice she wanted that day for the icebox: 25, 50, 75 or 100. When Mama put the sign in the window, she put the number that she wanted on top. Usually she wanted twenty-five pounds.

Mama kept lard and other food in the icebox. It had two long doors with chrome handles and several shelves, and it was taller than we kids were. But Mama didn't buy much food ahead of time because the icebox didn't do too good a job of preserving food. Instead, she went to the market every day.

When we saw the iceman coming on a suffocating St. Louis summer day, we kids quit what we were playing and raced for his wagon. We watched greedily as he chiseled off a twenty-five-pound block of ice for Mama, fighting over the chips of ice that flew from the block. What a treat ice was for us! The iceman carried the block of ice up the front stairs with big iron tongs. Then he lifted the lid of the icebox and set the ice in the tin-lined box. Mama always watched the pan under the icebox on the floor that caught the melted ice so it wouldn't overflow and flood the kitchen. While the iceman was upstairs, we grabbed small chunks of ice from his cart before he came back down and chased us away.

The milkman came through the alley and set our milk on the back porch right by the door. Milk was not homogenized then, so all the cream came to the top. Only a paper lid stood guard between the elements and that delicious layer of cream. In the winter the cream froze and rose up out of the bottle. If we didn't bring it in right away, the stray cats licked the cream off. So Mama tried to go out and grab the milk as soon as the milkman came, but sometimes he came real early in the morning before everybody was awake. Then the cats got to the cream first.

Once in a while we found a milk bottle in the alley, and that made us really glad. We washed it and put it out for the milkman, or we took it to the store and got a penny for it. Then we put the penny on the streetcar track and waited impatiently for the streetcar to come. After it rattled by, we raced to see the penny flattened out and very long. At other times, if we found a penny, we bought penny candy.

We kids were scavengers. We combed through the alleys and raided trash piles, looking for anything of value. It was just something to do, and sometimes we found something we didn't have. One day Claude found an envelope in an ash pit. When he opened it, he saw money inside—a ten-dollar bill! Claude pulled it out and whooped, "A ten-dollar bill! Oh, I never saw one before!" All the kids ran over to see it, wishing they had found it. "I'm going to take it to my mother," Claude announced. We all paraded home to Mama with Claude's find. Of course, word about something like that spread fast, and soon all the kids in the neighborhood heard about it and told their parents.

Claude showed Mama and Papa the envelope with the money. It must not have had a name or address on it, because the first thing Mama and Papa said was, "We've got to find out who it belongs to."

As the news of the find spread, a lady from down the alley came running to say it was hers. There was no way to prove it, so Mama gave her the benefit of the doubt. Some of us remember Mama giving her all the money, and some of us remember Mama giving her half the money because there was some question as to whether or not she was telling the truth. But we all do remember that we were sad because we thought Papa and Mama would finally have a fortune—a ten-dollar bill!

The ragman came regularly with his tired old horse and cart. He drove slowly through the alleys and sang out, "Rags, old iron. Rags, old iron." Then people ran into their houses and gathered the nails or rags or whatever they had to sell him. He bought anything, even old newspapers. His cart was always piled high with all varieties of junk.

Of course, he paid very little, but very little is more than nothing.

We kids picked up iron from around the railroad tracks, pieces of the train that rattled off or other pieces of metal we found. If we found a big piece of cast iron, that was a real treasure because we could get a few pennies for it.

One day when the ragman and his horse-drawn cart came down the alley, Claude remembered some iron rods he had seen on the lot next to us where the owner, a woman, was erecting a new building. She had reinforcing iron specially made to put in the concrete before they put up the building. Claude decided that those iron bars were a good source of money, so he sold them to the ragman for the tremendous sum of fifteen cents.

Well, a neighbor lady saw him do it, and she told Mama. When Papa came home and found out what Claude had done, he chased Claude down the alley for two blocks before he caught him. Then he took his belt off and gave him a beating. He whipped him all the way back to our yard.

The woman who owned them wanted two dollars apiece to replace the rods—twenty-eight dollars total. What a fortune that was to us! But

A Memory from Claude

The lady next door was building a new building. She had a bunch of reinforcing iron that she had specially made to put in the concrete before they built the building. I decided that those iron bars were a good source of money, so I sold them to the ragman for fifteen cents. Somehow or other, she found out and told Pop, and she said I had to go to jail. So Pop went to the blacksmith, Ben Moyer, and had these bars made up. He paid twenty dollars for them. We got out a lot cheaper than if he had needed to buy them new, but I got a lickin'.

Papa arranged with Mr. Moyer, the blacksmith, to forge new ones according to her specifications. Mr. Moyer only charged Papa twelve dollars. Who knows whether Claude knew he was doing anything wrong or not. He might have just thought, as kids do, that he had a clever stroke of luck!

Claude was always into something, and he often got caught. Once he really got caught—stuck between buildings! There was a small space between our red brick building and the new brick building next to it—the one the woman who owned the metal rods built. The space was narrow at one end and wide at the other.

One day when we were playing in the back yard, Claude said, "I know I can make it all the way between those buildings and come out the other side onto the sidewalk. I know I can."

"Claude, you better not. You might get stuck," we warned.

Well, that was all it took. He started out at the wide end and walked toward the narrow end between the two buildings, inching farther and farther. Then, wouldn't you know it, he got his head stuck just when he was almost through. He couldn't go forward, and he couldn't back up. Oh, did he cry! We ran and told Papa and Mama. Papa came to look the situation over, and he couldn't get Claude out. Neither could Mama. Of course, she clasped her hands and muttered, *"Eyou! Muka moya! Statche de radam sad?"* Such trouble. What should they do next?

The neighbors told Mama to call the fire department. In the meantime Claude was really blubbering because he thought he would be there forever, I guess. Pretty soon the fire department came. After lots of thought, the firemen came up with a clever idea. Somehow they greased Claude's head, and out he slipped! Claude was really scared, but he was so glad to be free again. All the kids on the block envied all the attention he got and the fact that a big red fire truck had come to our house!

Sometimes Claude drew a circle in the dirt so he and his friends could play taws. We called them taws then, but today they're called marbles. He found an old Bull Durham tobacco bag with a drawstring. It was worn and dirty, but Claude carried his taws in it. Claude was good at shooting the other kids' taws out of the circle. That's the way he got more. Claude hit with a two-bagger—a large shooter marble. I liked the two-baggers because they were big and had beautiful colors on them, like blue swirled with white.

Sometimes Claude was lucky enough to win an agate, which cost ten cents in the store. They were the kind of taws you would get a boy for a gift. I played taws once, but they didn't like girls to play.

After dinner in the winter we played games inside, such as Jack Straws or Truth or Consequences. Or we sat around and talked. Years later we acquired a radio, but we didn't have one at first. Sometimes in the evenings I recited poems to my family. All kids had to learn poetry at school. The teacher assigned us a poem and gave us a few days to memorize it. Then we each stood in front of the class and recited it. In the eighth grade I memorized wonderful poems like these, most of which I still know by heart:

"O Captain! My Captain!" by Walt Whitman
"A Psalm of Life" by Henry Longfellow
"Trees" by Joyce Kilmer
"Flander's Field" by John D. McCrae
"If" by Rudyard Kipling

Plus, I learned parts of President Lincoln's address: "With malice toward none, with charity for all…." We loved our country, and we loved to say so. We learned about decency, honesty and courage. Patriotism and honor pulled at our heartstrings. Everyone was moved when I recited lines about the soul, about treating our fellow man with dignity and respect, and about our great country. Papa was especially affected. When I recited "O Captain! My Captain!" he cried because he felt things deeply. He cried when the flag went by in a parade, or even when he was thrilled by something beautiful, like music.

After I learned to read, I read day and night. I went to the library all the time and brought books home to read. In the evening I read to everybody. They just loved it, and they couldn't wait for the next night when I would read the next chapter.

"Why don't you read us a story now, Millie?" they begged.

"No, we're going to wait until we eat and wash dishes," I said. I wanted the stage to be set, and that couldn't happen until all the chores were done. So after dinner when the dishes were washed, I sat on a little stool, and everyone sat in a semi-circle facing me. Whoever was holding the baby sat in the rocking chair. I read in the kitchen because that was the warmest room. The only light was the gas mantle light in the ceiling, but that was enough light because it had to be.

I read chapter after chapter of the new books I had discovered at the library. Papa and Mama were the most interested listeners. Mama just loved *Heidi*. In fact, once when she was in her sixties she asked me to read some of *Heidi* to her again. Papa loved *Robinson Crusoe* the best. Every time I read out of it, the next day he gave his men friends an update on the story. They liked to guess what would happen next.

Then I read *Pollyanna* to the family. Oh, everybody loved *Pollyanna*, and she did so many good things. She made everybody smile all the time. She said bright things when others said things that were depressing. Then there was *Rebecca of Sunnybrook Farm* and *Uncle Tom's Cabin* and *Little Women*. I loved them all, and I loved sharing them with my family.

When Bee Bee Caram told me about a wonderful book, I read it. Then I gave it to Ruby to read, and she read it too. Even today when I read a book I like, I mail it to Ruby and she reads it. Ruby wanted to learn everything too, and she read a lot.

Mama used to get angry with me when I read too much and didn't do my work. Instead I slid under the bed and read and read and read. I read all the time. How could I take the time to do mundane chores when so many exciting things were happening in the world of my books? I couldn't wait to see what would happen next.

I kept a Blue Jay notebook with the title and author of each book I read and the date I read it. I treasured the books I owned highly and kept them among my secret things. To this day I hide books I love in special places so if a burglar comes in, he won't find my true treasures!

When I began working, I didn't get a penny because I had to turn in all my money to Mama. That's what we all did, and we didn't resent it a bit. After a year or so Mama thought I should get twenty-five cents a week. So as soon as I got my pay every Friday

---

A Memory from Bee Bee

Millie is the one who got me to read. I didn't like school and I never wanted to read a book. I used to play and jump off the garage—I was a real tomboy. Millie was working, making practically no money at all, though I didn't know that at the time. She was helping the family. But she decided she wanted me to read. So she gave me a list of books and told me, "I'll give you five cents for every book you read on this list." Some books earned me ten cents, and a couple of books a quarter. Those were the hard ones, like Les Misérables *and* Anthony Adverse. *Once I started reading, I realized how wonderful it was. I read so much that we had to disband the money system because it wasn't working out very well for Millie, who didn't have very much to give.*

A Memory from Dorothy

I know Millicent read Mother Little Women *because I remember we all cried. Millicent wanted everybody to be educated. When I look back, I realize she was really so wonderful because she tried so hard. If we read a book, Millicent gave us a quarter. And if we memorized a poem, she gave us a dime. Millicent loved poetry and books. I learned "Trees" and a couple of other poems. But I wasn't very scholarly. I was always out playing some game. I wasn't the reader or the studious one.*

---

and came home and ate my supper, I ran down to the store around the corner and bought a Ruth Fielding book. She was my heroine. I read *Ruth Fielding in the Great Northwest, Ruth Fielding at Cameron Hall*, Ruth Fielding here, Ruth Fielding there. I read each book slowly to make it last till the next Friday when I could buy another one. I could hardly stand waiting to find out what happened next in the story, but it was worth reading it slowly to make it last longer. When I finished a book, I held it in my hands and looked at it and felt it. I was so proud to say, "I read this book." Reading was a great enjoyment for me as I met so many wonderful friends in my books, and I cried when I had to leave them.

I also read many fairy tales—*The Red Fairy Book, The Green Fairy Book, The Purple Fairy Book*—all of them. I was a fairy tale person. I believed in fairies. I always loved everything beautiful and lacy and fairylike. Papa contributed to that by telling all those grandiose stories and making us believe that the unbelievable could happen. So I had illusions of grandeur. I still have them today. I can't shake them.

Somehow, struggling immigrant families like ours found out about the free dental clinic at the St. Louis University school of dentistry on Grand and Rutger. We kids walked a couple of miles there alone to see the dentist. It was safe for a little girl to walk alone. At night or during the day—we walked everywhere and didn't give it a second thought. The students at the dentistry school filled our cavities for free since we could not afford to pay. Actually, they practiced on us, but they must have done good work. Even today, almost eighty years later, I still have some of those same fillings in my teeth. My dentist told me recently, "You may have gotten free dental work, but let me tell you, they did a good job."

One day I walked to the free clinic to have a tooth pulled. The dentist sat me in the chair, slapped something over my face and said, "Take a deep breath." That scared me so much. The mask seemed so big, and they didn't tell me what they were going to do. Almost immediately I was knocked out, and he pulled my tooth. When I woke up, my mouth was hurting and I was crying. But I started walking back home anyway. What choice did I have?

On the way home I looked up at the trees on the street near the dentist's office, and there among the leaves was a tiny fairy about two or three inches high! I stopped and watched her for a long time, almost not believing what I was seeing. She was a tiny person with wings, a beautiful pink dress and light, light hair. I stared at her and thought, *Oh, she is so beautiful.* I couldn't wait to get home and tell everybody about the fairy I saw.

I raced home filled with excitement and blurted out my story. But my family all laughed. "You've been reading too many fairy books," they said. I cried when none of my sisters believed me. No one on the block believed me either, but I knew what I saw.

To this day I know I saw a fairy!

Chapter Nine

Special Times

Even when people have very little, they still manage to celebrate special occasions and have good times. We were the same. In fact, these special events stand out in our memories more so than if we had been better off. Even small incidents tend to take on greater meaning when you're poor.

Once Mama went alone to Mr. Art Malone's jewelry store at the end of the block and told him she wanted to buy both Angie and me necklaces that we could have forever. She picked out some that were two dollars each. Mr. Malone was kind enough to let Mama pay him twenty-five cents every week, each time she received her pay for scrubbing Mrs. Barreta's house.

One day when nothing special was happening at home, Mama called for Angie and me. We could tell that she wasn't calling us to do a chore because there was an excitement in her voice. Angie and I came quickly because we were curious to see what she wanted. When Mama had our attention, she presented each of us with a smooth white box. I kept feeling my box because I had never received a gift in a box like that before. The box itself was a special gift to me. Finally I opened mine, and there inside was a beautiful necklace and earring set. My necklace was a lovely pendant on a gossamer silver chain. The pendant was set with an amethyst, my birthstone, along with tiny pearls, and the earrings matched. Angie opened her box to find a set like mine, but with blue stones.

"You're my two oldest girls," Mama said, "and I want you to have this jewelry to keep all the time, to wear and not lose, and to remember that your mother gave it to you." I had never seen anything so beautiful before in my life, and I couldn't believe it was mine to keep forever! I wouldn't let anyone else touch my jewelry—only look at it. I wore my jewelry once or twice, but I didn't wear it a lot because I was afraid I'd lose a piece.

My jewelry set is now in my safety deposit box at the bank. Now and then I go there and take it out and look at it, remembering how proud Mama was to be able to give us something to keep forever. Sometimes I bring it home and wear it around the house all day. Angie doesn't remember what happened to hers, but I saved important things like that. Even when I was a little girl, I saved things so that years later my friends could see them, and I could tell them the story.

I believe Mama wanted us to have the jewelry because she probably really loved the gold jewelry she had before she got married. But right after Papa and Mama married, Mama converted from Serbian Orthodox to Papa's religion. She became *verna*, or a convert to Protestantism. It was then that Mama quit wearing jewelry. Her religion taught that adorning yourself with jewelry was wrong, and Mama wanted to do what was right. She even worried about whether or not wearing a plain wristwatch was too ornamental!

When we were still in Canada, Mama gave all her jewelry to Angie and me to play with. Dorothy even remembers teething on it. I especially liked the shiny expansion bracelet. It was all gold, and I think Mama wore it on her wedding day. After a while we tore the bracelet apart and scattered the pieces around in the dirt, who knows where. All the jewelry she gave us ended up in pieces in the dirt around the farmhouse.

When we were growing up on Chouteau Avenue, Sunday was the only day Papa and Mama didn't have to work. It was the only day Mama had off, if you call having to take care of seven or eight children a day off. Sometimes on Sunday Mama arose at four o'clock in the morning and baked *kolatcha*. By the time we got up, the delicious smell of that butter cake was drifting throughout our two rooms.

We always had tea on Sunday afternoons. I guess Mama picked up that custom while living in Canada, where some of the British habits prevail. We had tea and donuts or *kolatcha* or bread with jelly at about four o'clock. I especially enjoyed this in the winter when it was cold and overcast and gloomy because it was a warm break.

But mainly Sunday was the day for church.

Perhaps Mama was so much more pious than Papa because she was a convert to the faith. Mama always wore a cap or a scarf on her head, as the Bible said a woman should have her head covered. She never cut her hair or wore makeup. But not many people wore makeup then anyway, just flappers—women who rolled their stockings down and wore short dresses and cut their hair into bobs. There was a popular song in the twenties called "Roll 'em, Girls, Roll 'em" that encouraged girls to roll down their stockings and "show your pretty knees."

Papa and Mama's religion came first. We always had a prayer before and after meals, and we all got down on our knees and prayed silently before getting into bed at night. I still do that even now. Even though I'm in my eighties, I'm still that little girl, kneeling down before God every night. Both Papa and Mama believed that prayer changes things, and they passed on those beliefs to us.

When Mama first arrived in Canada, she had fun and went to dances. She danced the Kolo, a Serbian folk dance. But after she converted to Papa's faith, she never danced anymore. Ironically, before they met and married Papa saw Mama dance once and thought she was beautiful. He was taken with the way her bosom went up and down when she danced. He once told Dorothy that's when he "fell in love" with Mama!

My grandfather, Daka, was one of the preachers at their church in Canada. When we moved to St. Louis, we children didn't go to church because Daka said, "Church is no place for children!" Later, after Daka moved back to Yugoslavia, we did attend Papa and Mama's church, but maybe Daka was right because it sure didn't appeal to us much as children.

The men sat on one side of the church and the women sat on the other—all on plain

---

A Memory from Stella

Mother's church had so many don'ts that it wasn't even funny. Don't cut your hair, don't wear make-up—well, they weren't going to keep a bunch of Petrov girls down. Mother was smart enough to know that if she tried to sit on us too hard, we'd go bad. And nobody really went bad because she was smart enough to let everybody spread their wings. When we wanted to join another church, she said that was fine.

A Memory from Ruby

Mama let me iron Mrs. Rameseri's dresses. When I pressed the top of her dress, I smelled the perfume that came out of the fabric. I thought that was so fantastic. We couldn't have perfume, even if we could have afforded it. The church wouldn't even allow wedding rings. They hardly let women wear belts because they didn't want the women's figures to show. But all the young people were growing up into pretty young women, and the church had to change. By the time Claude got married, they had finally started doing the services in English.

---

benches with no backs. From the second we walked into church, we had to sit quietly and not move. I sat next to Rose O'Moran. She and her family were some of our oldest and best Serbian friends. Rose was very strict, but I liked her so much. Actually, she was my mentor at that church. If I was making any noise, she put her finger to her lips as if to say, "Shhh." We tried to avoid going to the bathroom during church because the toilet was down in the basement. It made so much noise that everybody upstairs would know when we flushed it, and that was embarrassing.

When the preacher finished his sermon in Serbian, then another minister would preach in German, then another in English. Actually, they didn't start preaching in English until I was about fifteen. Before that, if you didn't understand Serbian or German, you were out of luck. The service lasted at least two hours, though it felt even longer. We got a little rest from the sermons when we sang songs. People had hymnals in their own languages—German, English, Slovak, Serbian or Hungarian. We all sang the same song, each in his own language. So all the songs were sung in five languages at once!

I didn't enjoy the services, but it never occurred to us to think about whether we enjoyed them or not. Going to church was just something we did. But we always got some joy out of going anywhere and seeing our friends.

A Memory from Dorothy

Mother was so devout and she so wanted to do the right thing. But all those manmade rules they had—it was such a shame because she was the most beautiful Christian I've ever known. Then to have all those terrible feelings that she was doing something wrong. Isn't that awful? She could have been a lot happier. I think she finally realized that God wasn't that small. I would tell her, "Mother, your God is too small." We had a lot of talks together, and I think she listened.

*A rare picture of Mama with us
kids in the park. Stella is the baby.*

Sometimes we went to the park after church in the summers. We played baseball with the other families. I thought I wasn't very good, and I didn't want to play most of the time. Sometimes they made me play, though. I'm sure I wasn't too bad, but I was so self-conscious and always thought that I couldn't do anything right. Angie didn't want to play either for the same reason, but everybody else in the family loved it.

Mama's church brought her great joy but also some sorrow. They didn't believe in setting a foot in any other church. So when both Dorothy and Stella got married at another church, Mama asked an elder of her church whether or not she should attend. She always tried to do the right thing. The elder responded, "What do you think, Mrs. Petrov?" He didn't want the responsibility of taking a difficult stand, but he left the impression in Mama's mind that going to their weddings would be wrong. So Papa walked the brides down the aisle, and Mama stayed at home, getting food ready for the receptions. Of course, Dorothy and Stella were crushed that Mama wasn't there.

Some years later that same elder attended his own daughter's wedding at another church. When Mama heard that, she said, "He didn't do what he told me to do." And later she told Stella and Dorothy, "I never should have even questioned it. I feel so bad that I didn't go to your weddings."

During the time Daka didn't allow us to go to their church, Mama let us go to a

Sunday school with some other children on the block. It was a storefront holy roller church two or three blocks from us on Chouteau Avenue. As soon as I heard that the people there were called "holy rollers," I was anxious to see what would happen there. But I never saw anything happen. I didn't understand why they called it a holy roller church because no one rolled around on the floor.

A Memory from Stella

We went to church in the morning, then home for lunch. Millicent and Angie would have the lunch ready when we got home. Then we went back to church from two o'clock to three. In the afternoon the older Dreste boys would go to Tower Grove Park and save a picnic spot. After church we all congregated, and everyone brought a basket. Mrs. Dreste always brought different kinds of fruit that we never had or cookies from the store. Mama always made cookies, so we never got "bought" cookies. We liked the "bought" cookies! We played baseball and drop-the-hanky with the church people and had a great time.

A Memory from Claude

We had three families in church who each had eight children— the O'Morans, the Drestes and the Petrovs. That made thirty people. So when we went to the park, we had enough to have a ball team, an umpire and spectators—all from just three families!

Instead, we all sat on different kinds of chairs, and a man prayed and told us stories about Jesus. We each were given a little leaflet, and everyone sang nice songs about Jesus. There I learned to sing dear old hymns such as "Jesus Loves Me" and "What a Friend We Have in Jesus." I thought they were beautiful songs! There was no piano, but I remember one lady had a voice as beautiful as the words, and everyone followed her as she led the hymns.

When they passed the collection box, we all wondered why people put their money into it. When we told Mama about it, she gave us two or three pennies to put in next time. As we walked there the next Sunday, we argued about which one of us was going to put the money in the box. Angie thought she should do it because she was the oldest. Claude thought he should because he was the man. Somehow we resolved our dilemma, and the pennies ended up in the box.

I don't recall going to the holy roller church very long, although we did go one Easter morning. Mama bought a bolt of material from Bumstead's Dry Goods store and made us girls dresses. She just laid the material on the kitchen table and cut it out. She didn't have a pattern. Then she held the material up to us, one at a time, to see if it was the right size and length. The dresses were all one piece, and each was made the same way—straight with sleeves, elastic around the waist and a little ruffled skirt. The material was lavender checked with white stripes, and we thought our dresses were heavenly!

When we walked into that holy roller church on Easter morning, I saw the others looking at us, and I felt as if they wished they could have our beautiful lavender and white dresses! But I'm sure they were looking at us strangely because all five of us had dresses made from the same bolt of material.

After we quit attending the holy roller church, we kids didn't go to church at all for several years. On those Easters, as soon as we woke up in the morning and finished eating, we rushed to Buder Playground. The teachers gave us baskets, then they put handfuls of chocolate-covered marshmallow eggs in them. We also got colored candy eggs and a chocolate bunny rabbit. That was a beautiful Easter to us.

The milk chocolate-covered eggs with the soft marshmallow inside were a treat that I remember to this day. Everywhere I go, all over the world, I keep hoping to find chocolate-covered marshmallow eggs like those, but I never have—although the marshmallow eggs at the old Mavrakos chocolate shop in downtown St. Louis were a close runner-up!

None of us remembers ever celebrating a birthday when we lived on Chouteau Avenue. I guess there were too many of us and too little money. When I was young I did go to a dance once. Papa was in charge of the dance—I don't know why. Maybe it was sponsored by the Patrons' Association. But Papa told Mama that Angie and I could go with him because we were the oldest. So Mama dressed us up in our nicest clothes. We took our best handkerchiefs and held them in our hands as daintily as we could. In those days all little girls had beautiful handkerchiefs that they cherished.

Papa took us up to the balcony and told us, "Now, sit here and you can watch everybody dance, and I'll be right downstairs." We sat there and scarcely moved. Occasionally Papa came up to see how we were doing. Once when he was checking on us, a lady in a beautiful dance dress came up to our table. She had been dancing, and she was sweating something awful. We could smell her body odor when she leaned over to say hello to us.

A Memory from Ruby

Mama made our dresses by hand until she got a treadle sewing machine, and she made them all alike. All us girls had the same color dresses, the same style—just a little larger for each one. She loved to smock, and she smocked all our little dresses, using green embroidery thread on pongee.

A Memory from Angie

We walked across the Compton Avenue bridge to show off our Easter dresses. When a steam train went under the bridge, we were standing in the way of the soot. We got back home and our dresses were full of soot. Did we get it!

Suddenly she said to Angie and me, "Let me borrow these a minute." We watched in horror as she took our precious handkerchiefs and wiped under her arms with them. I guess no one had invented underarm deodorant yet, because when she gave us back our handkerchiefs, they smelled horrible. We thought that was a terrible thing to do to our beautiful handkerchiefs! Poor Mama, she had to wash out those smelly handkerchiefs.

We did our best to celebrate Valentine's Day. They made some gorgeous Valentines in the twenties—lacy and frilly with cupids and hearts all over them. The expensive ones opened up into fold-out scenes. They were so beautiful they took my breath away. I always wanted to buy Mama a fancy Valentine like that, but we couldn't afford to buy those, so we made our own instead. We cut out pictures of children from the Sears-Roebuck catalog and pasted them on paper. Then we drew frills around them with Crayolas. Once we had some paper that looked like lace, and we cut it out and put it around the people in their Sears-Roebuck underwear.

The Fourth of July was always a grand holiday—not just for us, but for everyone. It was a very patriotic day. Every business closed. People really did remember and revere their country and their flag. We lined the streets for the Fourth of July parade, and when the flag went by, the men saluted. Everybody respected it. If a family had a flag—which, of course, nobody on our block did—they put it in their window. Parents gave their children small flags to wave. We all talked about how wonderful America was and how lucky we felt to be Americans. We wanted to do everything right to become better Americans and better people.

Sometimes we ended up with some fireworks on the Fourth of July. There was a flat cookie-shaped firecracker that we put on the streetcar tracks. Then we hid so the motorman wouldn't see us. We waited, eagerly peering down the street for the streetcar to come. When it finally went by, the firecracker popped, making a noise so loud that all the people on the streetcar got a scare. How we laughed and pointed at them, proud of our charade!

To me, the best of all the fireworks was called a "son of a gun." It was dark red and shaped like a small flat bottle cap. When we rubbed it against walls or on the sidewalk, it crackled and popped and sparked. It took quite a lot of rubbing before it was ground down to almost nothing. I can't find any now. I haven't seen them for years. Everywhere I see fireworks for sale I ask if they sell them, but no one does. No one even knows what I'm talking about!

Christmases were pretty bleak when we lived at 2943 Chouteau Avenue. Although our neighbors had pretty little Christmas trees, we never had any. The church didn't allow them. I guess they thought Christmas trees took the attention off Christ. But as we grew older, we kept yelling for one. Finally Mama and Papa consented to having a Christmas tree, but that was not until we were much older, in our teens.

Our first Christmas at 2943 Chouteau Avenue was the most meager. Since Angie and I were the oldest, Mama made us dolls out of clothespins. She felt so bad because she couldn't get anything for us. The next Christmas she bought Angie and me ten-cent dolls. She brought them home in a shopping bag, and we were so eager to see them, we could hardly wait

A Memory from Claude

At Christmas, we hung up our stockings. We got nuts and we got an orange, which was quite a treat. We always got a little candy cane too. Pop still used the age-old tradition that if you didn't behave before Christmas, you got a lump of coal in your stocking. And I was really mean then, a mischievous kid, until I was twelve, then I turned the corner. So I got coal sometimes.

till she opened the bag. How we cherished those dolls! Mama also bought a ten-cent set of dishes. When Papa told his boss at Famous-Barr, Mrs. Costello, about them, she gave him oodles of broken dishes instead of throwing them away. Then Papa patched them, and we had lots of dishes to play with.

On Christmas Mama always made cake so the day would be more special. Mrs. Dreste, a good friend of ours from church, brought over a basket of fruit and other good

A Memory from Ruby

Pop really tried to give us Christmas presents. He knew how much it meant, even though we weren't allowed to have a Christmas tree. We never had a tree growing up because of the church. Even though none of us kids joined the church except Claude, we were restricted by it. Our Christmases were very plain. That's why I like a tree so much now.

things to eat. The Drestes owned a grocery store, so they always had good things to eat. Throughout the year Mrs. Dreste brought over baskets for us, always covered with a cloth. When she came in, she chatted with Mama. We all stood around as politely as we could, waiting for her to give us permission to see what she brought. Soon she said, "Here, have some," pulling back the cloth. We helped ourselves to the bananas first. They were a special treat.

One Christmas we kids decided to try to get a whole bushel of coal for Papa and Mama as a Christmas present. In those days, bushel baskets were our grocery bags. We used them to carry everything. So there were always a couple of them rolling around in our back yard.

We waited for the evening train to come by. Then we all made faces at the engineer as the train slowed down to enter the Missouri Pacific roundhouse. We tried to make him mad at us. If he thought we were little urchins who were up to no good, he reached his long arm behind him to the coal pile, grabbed some coal and threw it at us. Gleefully we picked up each piece. After a few days of acting like this, we had enough coal to fill our bushel basket! We hid the big chunks of coal in different places all over the yard. Although Mama and Papa didn't come down the back steps too often, we didn't want them to see their present until Christmas.

When Christmas morning came, we were so excited! We told Papa and Mama that we had to go out into the back yard for something.

"It's cold. Don't go out now," Mama said.

But we didn't listen. "We'll be right back," we told her. Claude carried the empty bushel basket up to the porch, and one by one we brought the chunks of coal up the stairs and tossed them in. Then we covered the basket with a rag and dragged the bushel into the kitchen. Of course, we couldn't hurt the kitchen floor much because it was old wood. But we weren't thinking of how we were scuffing the floor. We were just so excited about our cherished gift.

We told Papa and Mama to close their eyes, then we took the rag off the top. When Papa and Mama opened their eyes and saw our gift, they cried to see all that coal. Papa always cried easily anyway, and poor Mama—she was so touched that we kids were aware enough of our tough financial condition to do something like that. After all, coal was twenty-five cents a bushel, and many times we were cold because Papa and Mama didn't have the twenty-five cents.

That was the first Christmas gift we gave to Papa and Mama.

Mama always made Serbian cookies at Christmastime. She called them sugar cookies, though they were almost a shortbread. Of course, she used lard in them, and each cookie was almost half an inch thick. We each received two cookies. I ate one of mine, then wrapped the other one and hid it away for my birthday on February 10. When I took my cookie out on my birthday and showed it to my brothers and sisters, they all wanted some of it. But I told them, "No! You should have saved one of yours too." That made sense to me.

Today all my sisters have this Serbian cookie recipe, and we bake them for our families during the holidays. But now we use butter instead of lard. Those cookies are a true part of Christmas to us.

Mr. Ed Weimer was an attorney who invested in Papa's first doll factory. Papa helped his wife, Ruth Weimer, with some type of expositions she had. Mrs. Weimer liked Mama so well, and Papa too, that she came to meet all of us children. I liked everything about her when I saw her for the first time. Her hair was almost blonde, and bobbed, and she was taller than Papa or Mama. I liked the nice, expensive-looking clothes she wore. She had a striped silk dress, similar to the one Bee Bee Caram wore. Was it beautiful!

And I was taken with the way she talked, using big words that I had never heard before. We thought Mrs. Weimer was so educated, and I guess she was. I told my sisters and brothers that I wanted to talk like her someday. I so admired people who could speak well, and I thought she spoke better than any of my teachers.

Ruth Weimer took the Petrov family under her wing. She was so kind to us. Each time Mrs. Weimer came she brought food and small gifts and some clothes for one or the other of us. Most of the time we went out to play after she arrived. When we came back in she was still there, talking with Mama. One day Mrs. Weimer gave us each three cents so we could buy ice cream cones. We ran to the confectionery on our block and proudly ordered the cones.

"Show me your money first," grumbled the man behind the counter.

When we put our pennies we had down on the counter, he grunted and reached for the cones, plopping a big scoop of ice cream on each one. We couldn't wait till our tongues tasted the delicious and smooth ice cream! By the time we walked slowly back home, we had eaten down to the tips of the cones. I looked into my tip, and there was a big black roach! Still, it wasn't easy to throw the tip away. To this day I never eat the tip when I eat an ice cream cone. I know I won't find a roach there, but somehow I just can't eat that tip.

One Christmas Mrs. Weimer brought us dried figs on a string. We took them off and ate them slowly one by one. She also brought English walnuts and some honey in a gray crock. It was the first time we had ever seen walnuts, so she showed us how to crack them. She had Mama pour some of the honey into a dish, then she showed us how to dip our walnuts in the honey. Oh, that tasted heavenly! Even now, when Christmas morning comes, I have to have English walnuts dipped in honey, for to me that is part of Christmas.

One winter Ruth Weimer asked Mama if Angie and I could go to a Christmas party her company was giving. Of course, Mama said yes. That night Mama dressed us in our best clothes. She borrowed some crimpers from a neighbor, and she crimped our hair.

She had never done it before, and she burned our scalp. But we were too excited to let that bother us.

Finally Mrs. Weimer came to pick us up. I was too thrilled to notice the ride there, so I don't remember if we rode in a car or on a streetcar. But soon we arrived at a large building and walked into a big open room with many other children. Angie and I stared at the Christmas tree with all the beautiful candles and glass ornaments and strings of popcorn on it. Our eyes grew very big as we gawked at everything. Most of the other children were just as dumbfounded as we were, staring at the wonder of it all. Red and green tassels hanging here and there, festoons and gay ribbons—it was just beautiful! We'd never seen anything like it.

We were asked to sit down on the floor, which we obediently did. Then Santa Claus came strolling in with his big red bag. He reached into it and found a package for each one of us. The paper that wrapped my package was so beautiful I didn't want to tear the present open. When I finally decided to unwrap it, I was very careful, because I was determined to take that paper home.

When I opened my gift, I saw the most heavenly blue sweater I'd ever seen. Instantly, I loved it so much. It had big blue buttons and even a belt with it. I put it on right away. Angie also got a sweater, though I don't remember the color of hers. She put hers on too.

After Santa Claus left, they gave us some delicious cake. We each received a pretty bag of cookies and beautiful hard candies that looked like ribbons. It was wonderful. We had never been to a party like that before. We didn't even know it was called a party.

When we got home, Papa and Mama and the other kids were waiting for us. No one wanted to go to bed until we came home to tell them all our stories, and we couldn't stop talking! We had our sweaters on, and we showed them off. Everyone thought everything was so beautiful.

We opened our little bags of goodies and shared the candy and the little cookies with beautiful red and green icing on them with everybody. They were so pretty we didn't want to eat them. In fact, we saved one for a long time just to look at it.

"How kind of those people to give things to the poor people," Mama said. "How kind it was of them." She had tears in her eyes. Years later I realized it was indeed a party for underprivileged children, which I guess we were.

Chapter Ten

Moving On

The year 1929 is remembered for the stock market plunge and the beginning of the Depression. In my little world it was a momentous year too.

Mama was pregnant again. She was cleaning for Mrs. Teuteberg, whose husband was a pharmacist. Their drugstore was on the corner at the end of the block, on Chouteau Avenue and Ewing. The Teutebergs rented the front two rooms above their drugstore to Dr. Garvin, who used one as a waiting room and one as an examining room. I guess Mrs. Teuteberg liked Mama, because one day she and her husband asked Mama if we

In 1932, at
age seventeen.

In 1934, at
age nineteen.

When moved away from 2943
Chouteau Avenue, I started
becoming a young woman.

In 1938, at age
twenty-three.

wanted to rent the back rooms upstairs that Dr. Garvin didn't use. Papa and Mama said yes, and they took us to see the place.

Oh, we thought we were really stepping up! To move to a flat with three rooms plus a big kitchen and an attic and beautiful hardwood floors—why, that was almost heaven! And it had electricity. All we had to do was press a button on the wall and light would flood the room! Best of all, there was a toilet upstairs in the house, so we no longer had to go outside to use the toilet.

We spread the word in the neighborhood that we were moving to this beautiful place, and our friends were glad for us. So in the spring of 1929, right after my fourteenth birthday, we moved from my beloved 2943 Chouteau Avenue to our new home at the end of the block, 1004 South Ewing.

A couple of months later I graduated from the eighth grade. Two or three days after I graduated, Mama and I were alone in the house. "Well, Millie," Mama said slowly, "I know you're going to be disappointed, but I don't know how you can go to high school. You have to go to work so the other kids can go to school." I know it was difficult for

Mama to tell me that. She probably tried to wait for the right moment, but there never was a right moment for news like that. Mama wished I could go to school. She knew I loved to read, and that education meant so much to me. I could see that she hated to tell me that I had to go to work instead.

I listened as Mama talked, and I didn't say much. As soon as she was finished, I felt really scared. It suddenly hit me that the my childhood was over. Left behind in that plain two-room flat at 2943 Chouteau Avenue were my innocent, carefree and joyful days as a child. Now they were gone forever, existing only in my memory.

I had never looked for work before, and I was bashful. I had never pushed myself like that. Going to strange places and asking for a job—that terrified me. But I accepted it. I would never have thought of rebelling. If Mama said I had to go to work, then I had to go to work.

Angie had already started working—first at a shoe store down the block, then at Nugent's Department Store in Wellston. Claude, Ruby, Dorothy, Jimmy, Stella and Bee Bee all got to finish high school. Ruby was the scholarly one among us. Too bad she couldn't go to college, but we couldn't possibly afford it. As Ruby says, we couldn't even afford the car fare to get her downtown to a university.

Claude worked for Mr. Teuteberg for a while after school, behind the soda fountain downstairs in the drug store. Mr. Teuteberg taught Claude how to scoop up the ice cream so that the inside of the scoop of ice cream was hollow. That way, each scoop used less ice cream. Claude didn't like doing that because, to him, it was cheating. He told Mama, and she thought it was wrong too. So Mama told him to quit.

A Memory from Stella

Ruby made great grades. She was vice-president of her class. In fact, she got more votes than the president, but they'd never had a girl president before, so the boy won.

Meanwhile, I started looking for work. Someone told me that the Kroeger Grocery and Baking Company not far from us was hiring girls in the cookie department. I was shivering in my boots on my way there because I had never gone into an office and talked to anybody about a job before. Did I look right? Would I talk right? Would I be hired?

When I got there, I saw a line of girls looking for jobs. So I got in line and signed up with them and was hired! They told us the work was six days a week, ten hours a day, and the pay was thirteen dollars a week. Then they took us to the assembly line and put us to work right away!

In 1933 I used twenty-five cents of my money to have this picture taken of Jimmy, Stella and Bee Bee.

I was thrilled, and when I got home that night and told Mama, she was surprised that I got a job so quickly. And when I told her my wages, she thought that was great too. I was so proud to be helping my family.

The work was monotonous, but I didn't know any different. As the plain cookies moved past me on an assembly line belt, I picked them up one by one and put them under a machine that added icing, which I spread out with a little trowel. Then I hurriedly put them back down on the belt so they would get to the next girl in time for her to put the tops on.

We were told, "You cannot eat any cookies!" But at our breaks, we were allowed to eat the broken ones. One girl had a large bosom, and she stuffed cookies in there to take home because she had a lot of kids. She took the risk and got away with it. But a different girl got caught hiding cookies in her bosom, and she was fired.

———⦅⦆———

A Memory from Claude

Because I was older, I fell into the category of the first two—Angie and Millie. They had to quit school, go to work and help support the family. Though I didn't quit school, I helped by having three paper routes. I didn't make much—about fifteen or twenty cents on each route. There were four papers in St. Louis at that time: Post, Star, *and* Times, *and then the* Morning Globe, *which came out at night.*

When I was about ten, I sold the Morning Globe *from about nine to eleven o'clock at night. There was one particular man who came to my corner every night and bought two papers, the* Star *and the* Times. *They were two cents each, and he always gave me a nickel. So I got a penny tip on him.*

Then I got up at four o'clock in the morning and got a big bundle of papers and sold them at the corner not too far from the high school. After school I went to another corner and sold papers at the bridge on the corner of Jefferson and Chouteau Avenue. That was the second best corner. You graduated from the worst corner to the next best one to the next best one. Of course, the guy who ran the paper routes would never give up the best corner. I didn't get much sleep. I turned all the money in to Mom so we could eat.

One morning, it was snowing real hard, with about six inches of snow on the ground, and I got dressed and started to go out. Mom looked at me and said, "This is the last time you're getting up this early and going on this route. Give up that morning route." And that was the end of that route.

———⦅⦆———

I only had that job for two weeks. My boss wanted the girls to flirt with him, and I didn't understand all that. I was completely ignorant about the birds and the bees. I rejected his advances, so I was fired.

The next job I got was at Frank and Meyer Neckware Company on Washington Avenue, doing piecework, getting paid for the number of ties I sewed by hand. Did I work hard to make as many as I could! There was no air conditioning, though there were fans in some areas. Today it would be known as a sweat shop. We could go to the bathroom once in the morning and once in the afternoon—at least, that's how I remember it. Maybe I took breaks so seldom because I was trying to make so many ties so quickly. I worked at a machine with a bare light bulb hanging over it that provided a meager amount of light. Years later I realized that affected my eyesight. Our forelady, Mrs. Cooper, was a big woman who was very strict. Everyone was afraid of her. She reminded me of Mrs. Proctor, my principal at Chouteau School.

As it turned out, I worked at the neckware company on and off for over fifteen years. It was a grinding job, but I was glad to be working.

Papa was still moving from venture to venture. He dove into one project, and when that didn't work, he started something new. But after we kids got jobs, whether or not Papa made a good salary wasn't as important as it used to be. Even though Mama was no longer working, our jobs provided more money than she was used to. Somehow Papa had more respect for us after we all started working. He treated us more like adults and was nicer to us. And Mama was so thrilled that we were all growing up to be the right kind of young men and women.

Soon Mama decided that we kids who were working could keep 10 percent of what we made for ourselves instead of turning it all in to her. I killed myself sewing neckties so I could make a little more money every week. The first week I received fifteen dollars in my pay envelope (we were paid in cash, never with a check). That meant I got to keep a dollar and a half for my own. I ran to Scruggs-Vandervoort-Barney with my dollar and a half in my pay envelope. There I put a down payment on a silver tea service for Mama—one with the tray, the teapot, the coffee pot, and the sugar and creamer. It was fifteen

A Memory from Angie

Eighth grade was all I got. I had my first job at fourteen—I told the guy I was fifteen. That was at the shoe store down the street. I worked from nine in the morning till nine at night selling shoes. I was so proud to take my whole pay home and give it to Mother. Later, when I worked downtown, Mama gave us 10 percent of all the money we earned plus car fare. She was very generous. I went to Union Market, and I came home with all of my money spent in vegetables. I read that vegetables were good for us and they made us strong. Later, when I worked for Famous-Barr in fabrics and sewing, I spent my 10 percent on fabrics and made the girls lovely things.

A Memory from Claude

I saved my extra money for when I got married. I had three hundred dollars when we got married. We bought a walnut finish bedroom set. It's upstairs yet.

A Memory from Stella

My first job was at Famous-Barr in the dress department where Ruby worked. She got me the job. I worked on Saturdays and made three dollars for the day. Dresses cost about three or four dollars. I saved the money Mama let me keep, and I bought myself a winter coat. It was seven dollars, a darling coat with a velvet collar, like a Chesterfield, as they called them.

dollars. I put it in will-call and paid fifty cents a week on it.

I wanted to give Mama something elegant and beautiful, something that only rich people had. I wanted to surprise her with something she never thought she could own, something she could keep all her life. Since I always had illusions of grandeur (which I got from Papa and the books I read), I wanted to get her something way above her means and her dreams.

Was I proud when I finally paid off that tea service! The sales clerk wrapped it up beautifully, and I carried it home. It was in a Scruggs-Vandervoort-Barney box, and that was a classy store. I hid the box until Christmas, then I presented it to Mama. She cried

---

A Memory from Jimmy

When we first started listening to a radio, it wasn't ours. We lived over Teuteberg's Drug Store, and they would have the radio on. Every Saturday night "Amos 'n Andy" came on. So we all put our ears to the registers where the sound came through, and we listened to "Amos 'n Andy." They turned it a little louder for us so we could hear it.

A Memory from Claude

After we got a radio, we listened to "Amos 'n Andy." That was the entertainment then. It came on every Tuesday night, and when "Amos 'n Andy" came on, everybody—I mean the whole town—listened. That was the main attraction. No matter where you went you heard "Amos 'n Andy."

---

when she opened it. "I never thought I'd ever have a silver set," she said. She never wanted to use it. She just had it sitting out. In those days people didn't want to use nice things. They just had them sitting out for others to see.

Times were changing, and so were we. We started to acquire a few things that other people had and enjoyed. Somebody gave us a tall Victrola while we lived on Ewing. Oh, how we loved to play records! We listened to the magnificent voice of Enrico Caruso, and we played a French song that we called "Oy, Oy, Marie." That's how we pronounced the title we read off the record label, "Oui, Oui, Marie." What did we know about how to pronounce French? We thought the song was so funny. We played it over and over.

We also owned a record of the Two Black Crows, who were two white comedians pretending they were black. I still remember one of their jokes: "I'll meet you at the corner at five o'clock. If you get there first, you draw a blue line. If I get there first, I'll rub it out." We thought that was hilarious. Papa and Mama laughed and laughed.

A Memory from Ruby

I patted Mama's belly and asked, "Why are you so fat, Mama?" But she just brushed it aside. She didn't tell us there was a nice little sister in there for us or we would have all started jumping up and down. You didn't say those things then. The night Mother started having her contractions, we were all sent away to a church member's house. Millie cried and cried because she knew what was happening. And when we got home, there was this darling little baby cradled in Mama's arms.

One day in the early fall of 1929 Papa was shining his shoes with a rag. He was dressed up, ready to go to a Republican meeting. Mama said something to him in Serbian, and he got so mad he threw the rag down and said, "Oh, for goodness sake. Now? Right now you have to have the baby? I planned to go to this meeting, and now I can't go!"

A Memory from Stella

When I was seven, I broke my arm at Chouteau School. They brought me home, and Dr. Garvin set my arm. Mama had just delivered Bee Bee the day before, and she was still in bed with the baby. So I hid behind the door so Papa wouldn't see me when he came home. I was afraid Papa would belt me one for breaking my arm. He went in to see Mama and saw me behind the door. All he did was ask me what happened.

Mama said she was hurting, so Papa told us all to go somewhere. Jimmy and Claude and a neighbor boy ran across the Eighteenth Street bridge all the way downtown, which was about three miles. Then they ran the whole way back. The rest of us were shuffled off to a friend's house. Meanwhile Papa got the midwife.

Just a set of pocket doors separated Mama and Papa's bedroom from Dr. Garvin's waiting room. So Mama tried not to scream while she was in labor! Finally we got the word that we could come home. When we all walked into Papa and Mama's big bedroom, we saw Mama with a baby.

Mama asked us what we thought we should name this new little sister. We all helped pick out her name, Bernice Ruth. We name her after my Greek girlfriend, Bee Bee Caram (Bee Bee is the nickname for Bernice), and after Ruth Weimer. So that's how Bee Bee, as we called her, came into our family.

Dr. Garvin gave Papa and Mama a generous gift of money as a present for Bee Bee, and they put it in the bank. But it got wiped out in the financial crash a month later in October 1929.

When Bee Bee was about three years old, we entered her into a children's beauty contest at a store on the block. We dressed her up in long white stockings, a smocked dress that Mama had made and a bonnet to match. We all knew that Bee Bee was the most beautiful baby in the world, and she would surely win!

Here is Bee Bee dressed for the baby contest, then at age seven.

A Memory from Ruby

Bee Bee was our doll baby, our mala sestra, *our beautiful little sister. We all loved her. We spoiled her to death. She came seven years after Jimmy, and we all felt so grown up compared to her. It was almost like having our own little baby. We just petted her all over the place. Bee Bee never crawled on her hands and knees. She sat on her little bottom and she scooted everywhere. She was so cute!*

A Memory from Jimmy

Papa made root beer as well as a little homebrewed beer, and Dr. Garvin used to come over and have some. He fed Bee Bee homebrewed beer just to see her reaction. She was in a high chair then. She took a drink and said, "Ahhhh!" Mama didn't like it at all, but Dr. Garvin could get away with murder because he took care of all of us for free.

When we arrived at the contest and saw how utterly modern the other babies were dressed, we were worried that maybe Bee Bee wouldn't win. The other babies had fancy store-bought clothes, and Bee Bee looked quite old-fashioned. Of course, when they selected the prettiest baby, it wasn't Bee Bee. We went home angry because we knew that Bee Bee was really the most beautiful!

On Ewing Papa made root beer—and beer too. Sometimes the bottles exploded in the closet because he didn't do something right. Once somebody was coming up the stairs, and Papa hurriedly pushed the beer under the bed because that was still during Prohibition. Papa sat with another man and drank some beer occasionally. But Papa was never drunk—no, never! We never even saw him what I would call "high" today. He never drank that much. We had sweet wine on Thanksgiving and Christmas, but nobody in our family ever wanted to drink.

Every day when Dr. Garvin walked up the stairs on the way to his office, he stopped by and put two bottles of beer in our icebox. In between patients he came back to our kitchen and sipped some beer and talked to Papa and Mama. Then, when a patient came, he put his white jacket back on and went to his office.

Sometimes Dr. Garvin needed a prescription filled for a patient, so he asked one of us kids to run downstairs to Teuteberg's drugstore for him. Usually Ruby ran down and got it for him, and when she returned, he gave her a few pennies or a nickel. She was his favorite, and once he gave her a wool bathing suit. Oh, Dorothy cried her heart out because she didn't get one. Dorothy was real skinny though, and Ruby was nice and plump. Everybody knew Ruby was the prettiest one of us.

About two years after we moved to Ewing, the Teutebergs decided they didn't want to rent to us anymore. We probably made too much noise running up and down the wooden stairs. So we moved five or six blocks away to 1920 Hickory, an upstairs flat with five big rooms.

On Hickory Mama gave me a dresser drawer all to myself. Oh, I was so thrilled. No one else could use it. That was the first time I had any space of my own—except when I hid under the bed. The other kids wanted to see what I had in my drawer, but I wouldn't let them look. Mama stood up for me. "No, this is only Millie's. You can't touch anything in it." My drawer was for all the things I saved, my very own place. In it I kept some books I loved, the list of books I read, Bee Bee Caram's letters from Greece and some photographs that Mama gave me for my very own.

One day someone invited Papa to go to a Republican meeting, where he met a woman named Mrs. Louise Brooks. She gave a talk, and he invited her to come home and meet Mama and all of us. Papa was very gregarious. He was always getting to know new people. Mrs. Brooks was an older committee woman

A Memory from Jimmy

When we lived on Hickory, me and some of the other little kids in the neighborhood all took a little wagon and went down to the Camp Spring Company where they made springs for cars. The company knocked the slugs out of nuts so the screws would fit through. We made our own slingshots, and we shot all the windows out of the hat factory across the alley with those slugs. We shot at one pane of glass until we shot all the glass out of that one pane, then we went on to the next. We couldn't get out of our back yards for the whole summer—that was our punishment. The neighborhood cops who walked the beat checked every day to make sure we never got out of our yards.

A Memory from Jimmy

We used to bum old tires from the filling station. Then we got up at the top of the alley and had some kids at the bottom of the hill. They waved when they saw a car coming just right, and we rolled that tire down the hill and hoped it would hit the car. In them days, you could ride a bicycle from Hamilton Terrace all the way to Wellston without even seeing a car. That's why they flagged us when a car was coming. We didn't hit too many cars. Tires were old and flimsy in them days, old skinny things—they couldn't have hurt a car hardly if they hit 'em. If one did hit a car, we ran like hell.

---

for the 28th Ward, the richest ward in St. Louis. Papa admired her greatly. Soon she was coming to see us often. She turned out to be instrumental in helping Papa mature.

One day Mrs. Brooks said to Papa, "Arthur, you have such a wonderful family. You've got to get them out of this neighborhood on Hickory. It is worse than Chouteau Avenue. You have to be in a nicer neighborhood so your children can go to good schools and learn more about life than what they see right here. You should move west."

Papa told her he'd like to do that, but he didn't have the money for a nicer home in a better neighborhood. That didn't put Mrs. Brooks off, however. She drove around and looked and looked till she found a house for us at 5973 Hamilton Terrace. After she found it, she went door to door there and asked the neighbors if they owned their homes and if the neighborhood was good. She wanted to find a wholesome neighborhood for us kids. Were we surprised when we found out the house belonged to Mrs. Moise, my fifth grade teacher from Chouteau School.

Mrs. Moise wanted fifty dollars a month rent, but we couldn't pay that much. Papa and Mama talked with her and they settled on thirty-five dollars a month, which was still more than we could afford. But we moved in anyway.

We always heard that just rich people lived in the West End, and now we were living there! How proud we were of our two-story house. It had four bedrooms and a bath upstairs, with a reception hall and dining room, a living room and a kitchen downstairs. Mama always wanted us to act properly, to not make anybody ashamed of us. She wanted us to keep our yard clean like the other people on the block did.

An older couple, the Servants (pronounced elegantly with the accent on the last syllable!), lived next door to us on Hamilton Terrace. We became so close to them that they asked us to call them Uncle Gordon and Aunt Lucille. They were cultured and we weren't. Uncle Gordon had retired from the *St. Louis Post-Dispatch*, and he often drove us out in the country and showed us the scenery. That was a big thrill for us city kids. Aunt Lucille was a large woman who was always teaching us things. She said to us, "Girls, remember this all your life: A woman's hair is her crowning glory." Since then I've always tried to keep my hair looking feminine rather than sporty. Once I went to her house to ask if I could use her phone to call a boy, Jimmy Tegethoff. "No," she told me firmly. "A girl doesn't chase a boy. She waits for him to chase her."

We cleaned house for Aunt Lucille on Saturday afternoons. Of course, Dorothy

A Memory from Dorothy

Aunt Lucille came to school one day when Ruby and I were at Soldan High School. We were both staying after school at GAA (Girl's Athletic Association). Aunt Lucille said, "Come on, girls, I want you to get dressed. I talked your mother into letting me take you to the movie." We couldn't go to movies for so long. It was a sin. And she said, "I've talked Mother into letting me take you to see Grace Moore in One Night of Love.*" She was so excited. We quit playing, got into our clothes and went with her. What a treat to see that movie, with the beautiful music and everything.*

never did because she always had to go to a sports activity. "Oh, I can't," she said. "I have to go to the YMCA to a tennis tournament" or "I have to play ping-pong in a match." So it was Ruby and Angie and I who got the benefit of Aunt Lucille's guidance while we were cleaning. She played symphonies and operas on the phonograph, and she told us the stories behind each opera. When she told us about Madame Butterfly, I thought the story was so beautiful that I cried.

Papa worked then for the city of St. Louis. When it snowed he arranged for the whole block of Hamilton Terrace to be closed to traffic. It was a long block on a hill. All of us kids and our friends spent the day sledding down the street on the snow. Sometimes we put ashes at the bottom of the street so we wouldn't slide onto the cross street. No one remembers Mama ever coming out with us. She always was inside working—ironing or washing or sewing. But everyone remembers sledding down the hill to Hodiamont Avenue. Oh, were we popular when that happened! To have a papa who could get the street closed—that was something!

In 1932 the Republican candidate, Walter J. G. Nunn, lost the mayoral election. The Democrat, Bernard Dickman, was inaugurated instead. Papa's boss told all the people at the city shop to be prepared to lose their jobs by the end of the month because the Democrats were coming into office. Well, it happened just as Papa's boss said it would, but Papa wasn't prepared.

Mama says those were hard times because only Angie was working. It was right in the middle of the Depression, and I was laid off occasionally from the tie factory whenever they didn't have enough business. This was one of those times. So I found odd jobs here and there, such as sewing pockets in men's suits for a suit company. What precision work that was—putting on the front pocket. Then I worked for a company that made leather jackets, and that was even more difficult. I had to sew the yoke of the jacket onto the back. Once the needle went into the leather, it left a noticeable hole. So I couldn't make a mistake.

Soon Papa got a job for fifty dollars a month with the WPA, the Work Projects Administration (or as Mama said, the PWA), but that was short-lived. Then he worked for the Census Bureau translating names. Eventually Papa went to Soulard Market and bought vegetables wholesale. Then he took the back seat out of his 1927 Buick and put the produce in there. He drove up and down the alleys in our neighborhood and sold vegetables. According to Claude, that Buick had tires with wooden spokes, and in dry weather the spokes squeaked. So Papa poured water on them, and the spokes swelled up and the squeaking went away.

Later Papa rented space at Soulard Market on Saturdays to sell his vegetables. Stella and Jimmy and even Claude helped him. Papa sent Stella home early on the streetcar with two chickens—either alive or freshly killed. She was so embarrassed. The combination of the odor of the streetcar and the chickens in her lap made her sick. Mama would meet her at the streetcar with a paper bag because she had to throw up!

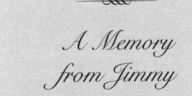

A Memory from Jimmy

I remember the biggest money-making day we had at Soulard Market. My dad bought one of the warehouses out of cucumbers. If I'm not mistaken, we made about $125 that Saturday, which was unheard of. Making $30 to $35 was a big day. We fed the whole neighborhood with cucumbers, and everybody was making pickles for the next week.

Once Papa traded the produce he had left at the end of a selling day for a bushel of sweet potatoes to bring home. By that time I was working again, and so was Claude. For days I took sweet potato sandwiches to work.

From Hamilton Terrace we moved a few streets away to a three-story house with a turret in the 5800 block of Etzel. We loved that house because it was so roomy and stylish. I shared a room with just Angie! One night when I went to bed, Papa pulled down the top half of the long window so we could get air. There were no screens on the windows. Angie came home late, and when she turned the light on, she saw bats flying around in our room! I was so terrified I got under the mattress and the box springs! Papa came in when he heard us yelling and chased the bats outside somehow.

The basement floor on Etzel was dirt, and rats lived there. Mama had to wash clothes down there, but it was muddy. Though the landlord promised to put a cement floor in the basement, he never did. So after three months we moved again. It was time to buy a home anyway. Mama was tired of moving.

Mr. Gradwohl, who had a jewelry store downtown, was selling his big house at 5958 Plymouth Avenue for four thousand dollars. Well, that was a great deal of money. Dorothy remembers that it was Mama who talked the Gradwohls into selling it to us.

Mama and Papa around 1936.

Evidently, they felt so sorry for her, they gave it to us for nothing down— just fifty dollars a month, with a balloon note due in three years. So in 1937 we moved into a lovely three-story red brick home with an attic, a basement and a large yard on Plymouth Avenue!

Later when the balloon note came due, Mama and Papa decided to refinance the house. According to Stella, Papa refused to pay the extra three hundred dollars refinance charge because he didn't understand it, and a policeman appeared at our door and took Papa to jail. Everything was finally straightened out, and Papa paid what he owed. When they redid the paperwork for the new note, Mama insisted that her name be added to all the papers. It was a good thing she did because that gave her the authority to refuse to sell the home to finance Papa's last doll factory in Illinois.

How I loved the dining room on Plymouth Avenue! It had carved wood wainscoting, with a shelf all around the wall near the top where we showed off plates. Mama tended her plants in the bay window in the dining room. Years later I descended the staircase to the strains of "Here Comes the Bride" and was married at that bay window.

When we first moved in to 5958 Plymouth Avenue, Mrs. Givens, the lady next door, didn't like us. She thought a bunch of gypsies had moved in, and I guess she was right. She reported us a couple of times for noise. But later on when Mrs. Givens got acquainted with Mama and Papa, she found out what good people we were in spite of all the noise we made, and we became good friends.

Claude put up five dollars to help Jimmy start a model airplane shop in the basement of our house. After a while Mrs. Givens turned Jimmy in for running a business in a residential district. When he had to close shop, he

Our grand three-story brick at 5958 Plymouth Avenue.

Bee Bee, Stella, Jimmy, Dorothy, Ruby, Claude, Millie and Angie outside our dining room bay window in the back yard of 5958 Plymouth Avenue, soon after we moved in.

Stella, Millie, Dorothy and Bee Bee
at our front door on Plymouth.

had turned that five dollars into five hundred dollars' worth of stock! He made so much money that summer he bought himself an ice cream almost every night!

All of us girls sewed our own clothes. But sometimes, when Kline's and Sonnefeld's each had their big sales, we all went there, even Mama. They sold dresses for two and three dollars each, and we bought armloads. The saleslady who always helped us went around and gathered just what we wanted. Then we went home and tried them all on, each of us choosing the dresses we liked. We hemmed or altered them as necessary because we could all sew beautifully.

We four girls stayed together in the upstairs front bedroom. Since we all shared the same closet and the same clothes, the first one up was the best dressed! The guys told us that from the back, they couldn't tell us apart!

Bee Bee and Stella shared another bedroom. But Bee Bee was messy and Stella was neat. So Stella hung a string across the room so people could tell whose side was whose. Stella remembers getting so mad at Bee Bee's mess that she showed Bee Bee the Christmas present she got for her ahead of time just to spoil the surprise.

When Claude got home from work, and I got home from my job, we sat and worked together on a hook rug. Angie bought the rug frame at Famous-Barr when she worked there, and Claude and I took turns hooking the strips of cloth through. As we worked, we talked and talked for hours about everything, as best friends do.

One early December day in 1941, a few of us were in Papa and Mama's bedroom ironing. We had the radio on, and the program was interrupted for this announcement, "The Japanese have attacked Pearl Harbor, Hawaii, by air, President Roosevelt has just announced." Where was Pearl Harbor? We had no idea. Why was it so important? It was so remote to us. But the next day President Roosevelt asked Congress to declare war on the Empire of Japan. How little we knew then what an impact that would have on our lives—and the lives of all Americans.

The four Petrov girls: Dorothy on top, Millie, Angie and Ruby.

Jimmy in his Navy uniform.

Once someone invited the four of us—Angie, me, Ruby and Dorothy—to the young people's group at West Presbyterian Church. Of course, we made a great sensation everywhere we went. People at the church called us the Four Musketeers. There we enjoyed hymn sings and Bible classes and hikes. And we met loads of boys there. I don't remember many girls, though. During the war we invited many servicemen over. Mama let us invite anyone we wanted to Sunday dinner, and our table was often crowded with boys!

Jimmy joined the Navy before he was drafted. Oh, how Mama cried! He went in the February after Pearl Harbor and served in the South Pacific. He won so much money gambling that he set up a table right next to the pay table. The sailors received their pay, then they lined up at Jimmy's table to pay him. He wanted to send the money he made to Mama, but she'd know it was from gambling, so he never did. Dorothy says that when Jimmy came back from the Navy, he looked just like Tyrone Power in his uniform.

Claude married Antoinette Dreste and was drafted in 1943 when their first son was only three weeks old. He had joined Mama's church by then—the only one of us who did. Since Claude was a conscientious objector because of his religion, they made him a medic in the war. There were lots of men then whose religion didn't allow them to carry a gun or shoot anyone. Oh, he had some awful jobs in India and all over Southeast Asia— treating the wounded and carrying the dead.

Claude in his Army uniform.

Papa got a position with the forestry department in Forest Park and learned about trees. Then (because he never liked to work for anyone else) he started his own tree trimming business. When Jimmy and Claude got back from the war, they bought Papa's tree business for twenty-five dollars, which included some saws and a Ford dual wheel pick-up truck. The tires were so worn on the truck that the cloth was coming through. But Papa said, "That's okay. They are ten-ply tires, and only four are gone. There are six ply left!" Petrov Brothers Tree Service is still in business today. Claude's sons run it, so it's still the Petrov Brothers—just different brothers!

Jimmy and Claude started Petrov Brothers Tree Service after the war.

Dorothy met a great guy named Charlie Moeller. Every one of us adored him. Oh, how we loved Charlie! He was a friend, a pal—so easy to know. He talked to everyone and was interested in all our problems. He just dived into the family and became part of us. Dorothy and Charlie married, then he was drafted by the Army. Near the end of the war Charlie was killed at the Battle of the Bulge. That was one of the most devastating blows ever to our whole family. Papa especially loved Charlie, so much so that Papa's black hair started turning gray immediately after Charlie died.

Dorothy was the first of us to work for McDonnell Aircraft. She was hired as a secretary. That's where she met Ned, whom she married after the war. During the war I worked there too, in a plant on Lindell that used to be an auto dealership. I worked in the tool-and-die division, making templates for airplane parts. Papa worked at McDonnell too, after the war. If not for the eight years he spent there, he wouldn't have received any pension at all.

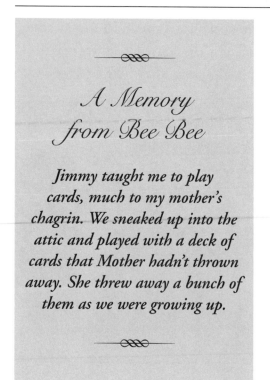

A Memory from Bee Bee

Jimmy taught me to play cards, much to my mother's chagrin. We sneaked up into the attic and played with a deck of cards that Mother hadn't thrown away. She threw away a bunch of them as we were growing up.

Mr. McDonnell was running the company. One day at noon Mr. Mac walked through the plant and said to all of us, "I think I'm going to get a big government contract, and I'm going to sell stock. I want to offer it to my employees first. So any of you who would like to buy stock, come to the office." Well, when he left the room, we all laughed. A few of us said, "Oh, he'll never make it." Many of us didn't even know what stock was. Stock was for rich people. So I never even considered buying any!

Stella met a wonderful young man at West Presbyterian, Lyle Gault. Mama really liked him, and so did we all. He sang beautifully, singing solos at church. He was always smiling and laughing. Stella married Lyle, and he became one of the family right away.

In the back yard on Plymouth we had a screened-in gazebo. Angie used to sit out there and talk with Milton Hamingson, her future husband, and do hand sewing. When she needed to put her needle down for a minute, she stuck it through her blouse into her bosom! Milton's eyes grew large as he stared. He didn't realize she was wearing falsies!

Bee Bee spent her high school years on Plymouth. She had lots of girlfriends, and sometimes she tagged along with us on our dates. We spoiled Bee Bee because she was so pretty and she was our baby sister. Once she went on a double date and fell in love with the other girl's date. Bee Bee and Joe were married when Bee Bee was nineteen.

As for me, I learned more and more as I worked for different companies and met people from all walks of life. Ruby talked to a fine young chiropractor every day on the streetcar going to work. She told him that her sister Millicent was the girl for him. So one day he came over to meet me. It was an instant attraction which lasted five or six years before the war separated us, taking him to England and me to Cincinnati to learn cash register repair. We never got back together. Two or three years later I was asked to teach arts and crafts at the USO in St. Louis, and there I met the man I married in 1947. We had two children, a boy, Charles Michael, and a girl, Christina. However, after twenty-nine years we went our separate ways.

After we settled into 5958 Plymouth Avenue, Ruby got a job with the Bell Telephone Company as a telephone operator for $12.50 a week. Stella remembers that Ruby had a three-to-eleven shift. We all had to take streetcars to work and back, and Ruby got to know her streetcar driver well. He would see her come out of work at eleven and wait for her. Instead of letting her off at the corner, he stopped right in front of our house, then

A Memory from Dorothy

Ruby was beautiful, and she was such a good dancer. She had beautiful clothes, and I wore them, then I wouldn't iron them. She got so mad at me because she always ironed her clothes after she wore them so they'd be ready the next time.

A Memory from Angie

Millicent, Dorothy, Ruby and I were all working at the same time. Ruby got up early in the morning and hid the suit she wanted to wear under her covers because whoever got up first got the best-looking suit. We were all close to the same size so we could wear the same clothes.

Stella, Bee Bee, Millie and Dorothy
clowning on Charlie's car in the driveway.

waited until she got in the door before he drove on. That's how considerate people were.

Ruby managed to get us a phone number that matched our street number: CAbanne-5958. She always had good jobs because she was so efficient. She was working as a secretary when she married Johnny.

We moved into our home at 5958 Plymouth Avenue in 1937 when I was twenty-two, and most of us lived there until we married and moved away. Young people lived at home then until they married. Our delightful years as young adults were spent in that big three-story house.

We grew up at 5958 Plymouth Avenue. Most of the Young People's group at West Presbyterian Church considered it their second home. Mama made platters of her home-made doughnuts, and they were gone in minutes. At 5958 Plymouth we met our boyfriends—and traded them, then dramatically broke up with them. That's where we rode in their Model A coupes and Duesenbergs and Cords, and sometimes we carried our friends in the rumble seats. There we met and married our husbands, and we had our wedding receptions in the huge back yard.

Papa grew up along with us on Plymouth. He had fun with us and our friends, and he realized we were all getting as smart as he was. On Plymouth Mama started sticking up for herself, Bee Bee blossomed and Mama tried to hold her down. In the driveway of

5958 Plymouth, Jimmy spread out all the parts of Model Ts and Model As and old Packards, then somehow put them all back together again. On Plymouth, Claude joined Mama and Papa's church and eventually became a minister. At 5958 Plymouth Avenue we girls held together during World War II, growing our Victory gardens and working in defense plants making ammunition and airplane parts. We watched our friends and boyfriends go off to war—and sometimes never return.

Oh, how I would love to tell all the things that happened at 5958 Plymouth! But that's another story.